As a professor, mento
set the standard for e.
helping professions. His dynamic and endearing teaching style
has ignited my drive to embrace his contagious passion for helping others. His touching and oftentimes lighthearted storytelling
based on real-life situations has helped me to comprehend the
heart and soul of counseling as opposed to just reading solely
from a book. He has not only helped to enhance my counseling
skills, but he has also given me continuous guidance and support
in my own personal growth. His caring and concern for his students' well-being has generated a positive and lasting influence
on many of our lives. His cognitive-based approach in working
with substance abuse has inspired me both personally and professionally. I can graciously attest that changing your thinking can
and will change your life. I am grateful to have had this inspirational man cross my path through this journey of life.

—Stacey Pattison
Central Michigan University faculty member

Dr. John Farrar is one-in-a-million teacher who is able to relate
to his students on a personal and professional level consistently.
He is my inspiration for pursuing my master's degree. As an
undergrad, I had the privilege of taking my first graduate-level
course with Dr. J., and I had never had a more fulfilling educational experience. His use of anecdotes and personal experience
are his greatest tools for teaching students to be congruent in
their thoughts and responses. He cleverly provokes interest and
student involvement with his engaging manner, quick wit, and
wry sense of humor. He gave me the courage to overcome personal obstacles to pursue my life goals.... Dr. Farrar brings personality, inherent wisdom, and his own personal mission in life to
his teaching and counseling.

—Brenda Gaeth

Dr. J., I want to thank you so much for all that you have done for my daughter. When I think back to the time when I tearfully approached you about what she was going through, I cannot believe the change in her! I don't know what her father and I would have done without your help and guidance. You were our "knight in shining armor" for her at a time when she desperately needed someone to talk to and help her through a rough time in life. You certainly picked the right profession because you are patient, kind, compassionate, and most of all, understanding.

—M.M.

Dr. J., I wanted to let you know that I made the hardest decision ever and chose to cancel the wedding. I know that it is the wisest decision at this time for both J. and me; however, feelings leave me brokenhearted. I keep telling myself, as you said, it will only get better each day. Thank you for giving me the courage and the tools to work through this most difficult situation.

—K.

Dr. Farrar, I would like to express gratitude for your professionalism and caring mannerisms. As you certainly understand, these addiction issues are emotionally draining, and it helps to have a person like you provide a stabilizing perspective.

—G.M.

Dr. J., As you know, I am alcoholic and have been through a series of personal relationship disasters. Since I began counseling with you, I am proud to say I received my two-year sobriety token, fulfilled all drug court expectations, and am determined to involve myself in a positive, healthy relationship. Thanks so much for helping me get my life back on track.

—C.M.

dump the
neanderthal;
choose your
prime mate

dump the neanderthal;
choose your prime mate

6 Reasons Women Make Poor Relationship Choices *& 6 Strategies* to Avoid Them

Dr. John V. Farrar

TATE PUBLISHING
AND ENTERPRISES, LLC

Published by Tate Publishing & Enterprises, LLC
127 E. Trade Center Terrace | Mustang, Oklahoma 73064 USA
1.888.361.9473 | www.tatepublishing.com

Tate Publishing is committed to excellence in the publishing industry. The company reflects the philosophy established by the founders, based on Psalm 68:11,
"The Lord gave the word and great was the company of those who published it."

Book design copyright © 2012 by Tate Publishing, LLC. All rights reserved.
Cover design by Erin DeMoss
Interior design by April Marciszewski

Published in the United States of America

ISBN: 978-1-61862-150-4
1. Family & Relationships / Love & Romance
2. Self-Help / Affirmations
12.01.23

dedication

Dedications are generally written for those who have assisted the author in some way. Perhaps it is the gift of encouragement or inspiration or guidance. In my case, it was something much more significant: the gift of a life.

This work, therefore, is dedicated to my wife Anita. She has been the source of everything good that has happened to me. I owe a family, a career, and this book to her beauty, her brains, and most of all her perseverance with a grateful partner.

acknowledgements

No author operates in a vacuum. At least this one didn't. Certainly the greatest acknowledgement for this book must go to my personal and professional partner of over forty years, Anita Farrar. My wife is also an LPC (licensed professional counselor), a skilled clinician in her own right, and a respected professional educator. More importantly for this effort, she is the most knowledgeable grammarian I know. Her input throughout this project, both technically and creatively, allowed this book to be completed in a readable fashion.

I also must thank my two children John and Christina. I have truly been blessed with two incredible, attractive, and intelligent children. As an educated, witty, and beautiful woman a generation younger than I, Christina was able to give me insights into the psyche of capable, young women, allowing me to better understand the information which the respondents to my survey and inventory provided. On a more personal note, Christina also provided me with the gray hair that enabled me to present a more distinguished presence to my students and clients as a result of some of her earlier dating misadventures. I also want to thank my fine son-in-law, Brad Vance, for being a trusted and caring husband to my daughter, also allowing my hair not to turn pure white and fall out. My son I must acknowledge for his unfailing encouragement and support. John is a tremendously successful businessman. An honorable young man as well, I am very proud to share his name. His respect and faith in me motivates me to strive to become the man he believes me to be.

A special thanks goes to Dr. Dick Fox, the former chair of the counseling department at Central Michigan University. Literally doing a cold call by walking into his office over ten years ago in search of a full-time faculty position, Dick had the confidence in me to give me a job. He has remained a valued mentor and friend ever since.

I also want to extend a thank you to Kelly Martin, a former graduate student of mine. Her work in the role that hormones play in influencing female mate selection motivated me to research that topic in greater depth for this book.

Most importantly, I must thank the over 300 women and girls who contributed to this study. They are, in many ways, the true authors of this work. Their willingness to share their difficult and, at times, painful stories made this book possible. I understand that they shared their stories as a personal catharsis, but also in the hope that their experiences might benefit other women who are navigating through the challenging waters of partner selection. Although there were over three hundred surveys completed, some of the surveys were incomplete. Given this fact, I based the data on the 259 fully completed surveys. All were done individually and in private. Respondents were all voluntary participants, having self-selected based upon their past relationship choices and situations.

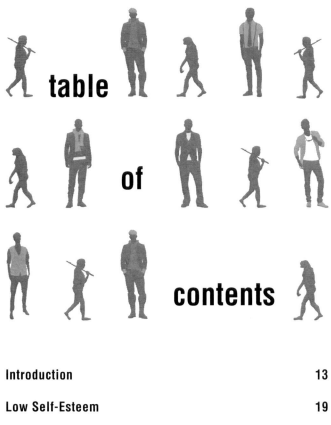

table of contents

introduction

Life is the sum of all our choices.

—Camus

Several years ago, a young student in my graduate-education psychology class asked to speak with me about a personal matter. She tearfully explained, "I know that you said your private practice is in an office with lawyers; I wonder if you could refer me to one." When I asked her why she needed an attorney, she mournfully narrated the following tale. "When I was sixteen, I had a job as head usher in a movie theatre. I started dating this guy who was one of my ushers. He was cute, older, and had a nice car. And I guess I was flattered that he was interested in me. We went together for a few years, and eventually I got pregnant. I have a three-year-old daughter now, and I'm in your class because I'm trying to get my life together and become a teacher. I broke up with my old boyfriend, my daughter's father. He got to be physically abusive, and I need a lawyer to help me get some kind of restraining order. I don't want him around either our daughter or me."

My young student went on to explain that early in her relationship with her daughter's father their life revolved around two destructive patterns: alcohol and unprotected sex. "He'd pick me up from school, buy a bottle, and we'd go back to his apartment." After she became pregnant at nineteen while a college freshman, she recalled, "He became progressively critical of me. He didn't want me to spend time with any of my friends, and he hated my parents." Shortly after the birth of their daughter, the couple split up with joint custody of their daughter being established via court decree, largely through the efforts of his parents. "Now I need a lawyer to get that decision reversed. He doesn't pay child support, and I think that the only reason he comes for her is to be able to spy on me."

The above story may sound extreme, but is only a somewhat more serious version of a pattern that I have encountered numerous times as a clinician and educator. I sometimes refer to this phenomenon as the *loser boyfriend* syndrome, and it appears to cross all age, ethnic, and soci-oeconomic lines. More descriptively, the pattern is one in which females of virtually any age, from teens to seniors, attach themselves to males who are significantly less capable, achieving, or functional than they. It has also been my professional observation that the reverse pattern, that is, men becoming involved with less functional women, does not appear to occur at anywhere near the same frequency.

In essence, we are looking into the classic dysfunctional relationship. The term *dysfunctional relationship* has merged into the category of a cliché. Sadly, it has become common for individuals to assert that there is no such thing as a "normal family; that all families are in some way or other, dysfunctional. I would humbly disagree. As a product of one of those clichés, I'm reminded of the classic remark of Justice Potter Stewart from the US Supreme Court in 1964 when commenting on a case dealing with pornography. He remarked that it was difficult to define hard-core pornography, but Justice Potter observed, "I know it when I see it." I would suggest to the readers of this book that those who grew up in a dysfunctional family know, at least by the time they hit their adolescent years, that their home life was not normal or healthy.

Having said that, I'll attempt to do what Justice Stewart struggled with by forming a definition or at least explain what a dysfunctional relationship is. I believe that the central characteristic of a dysfunctional relationship revolves around the concept of imbalance. A healthy relationship, conversely, reflects symbiosis. Both parties help and support each other. Their roles are not identical, but they are similar in terms of degree of effort. She may pay the bills while he maintains the home's grounds. Or she may work outside the home while he attends to more domestic duties. But each has a role which is balanced in terms of the amount of time, energy (both physical and emotional), and thought that they invest in that relationship.

The image of the Neanderthal was chosen for the title of this book because it seemed to epitomize the notion of an insensitive, thoughtless and, perhaps at times, an even brutish partner. Neanderthal-like behavior may not necessarily be physical, but it is always discounting of the wishes and feelings of his partner. A dysfunctional, unhealthy relationship does not exhibit either fairness or balance. The Neanderthal-like male says whatever he feels like saying, while she carefully watches her words. She does the cooking while he does all the eating. He abuses, and she gets abused. And so on. There is an imbalance in both effort and power. While she may be the breadwinner, for example, he may control the finances. She may work harder than he does to be sexually attractive, but he dictates their physical life together. As a result, the woman in these relationships manifests the stereotypical emotions of guilt, frustration, and mental exhaustion.

So, why is it that so many women find themselves in this sad state? That query lies at the core of my research into this phenomenon. To investigate this question, I have counseled and surveyed girls and women over the past several years. My respondents have ranged in age from sixteen to sixty, from high school girls to graduate students to professional women. My investigation has led me to the identification of six causes, or *strands* as I identify them, that lead to these relationship decisions. I refer to them as strands because there appear to be many *fibers* which combine to produce the motivational *rope* embodied in that strand. In addition, often women have been able to point to more than one motivation or strand that generated her relational choice.

I have also devised an inventory aimed at assisting women in identifying their tendencies vis-a-vis relationships. This inventory may also be used as either a diagnostic or prevention tool. It may be useful for young girls, perhaps under the supervision or monitoring of either parents or grandparents, to complete this instrument in order to identify personal tendencies or inclinations. (See Personality Profile.) In either case, the goal and purpose of the instrument is to serve as a *metaphorical mirror* into which women look for self-understanding and enlightenment.

Hopefully, the following chapters, case studies, and related basic principles of counseling and psychology will prove to be useful for the intelligent, caring, and dynamic women who have served as the inspiration and motivation for this work.

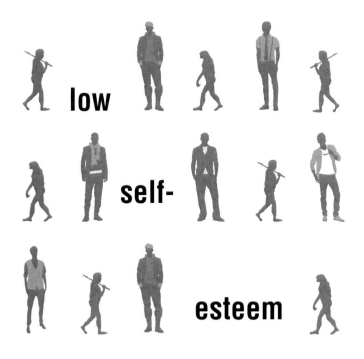

low self- esteem

Low self-esteem is like driving through
life with the hand-break on.

—Anonymous

Case Study: *Terri*

Terri sat quietly in my waiting area as I concluded a session with a client who had the frustrating tendency to raise the most important issue of the day during the final five minutes of the appointment. I introduced myself to Terri and extended my hand. She meekly took it while smiling nervously and avoiding eye contact. She chose a seat which was farther away from mine than most clients select. She avoided eye contact as she began to explain her reason for making an appointment.

Terri was a tall, lean woman—perhaps five-foot seven inches or five-foot eight inches in height. She was conservatively dressed and presented herself in a well-groomed but almost austere fashion. While she appeared to wear little or no make-up, her Nordic features and high cheekbones were reminiscent of a waif-like Audrey Hepburn.

"My girlfriend said that you might be able to help me." Terri then narrated that she had been married for eleven years. Her husband was a laid-off auto worker who has been receiving benefits at a rate of almost ninety percent of his original pay for the past five years. "Bob says that it doesn't pay him to go back to work. He hopes that he never gets called back." She stated that her reason for seeking counseling was to explore "ways to be a better wife."

Terri reported that they have no children, a source of disappointment to her. "I guess there must be something wrong with me, although the doctors can never find anything when I've been checked out before. Bob refuses to go for the tests they recommend." She turned away as she tearfully confessed that their sex life had declined substantially over the past several years. "It seems like he's lost interest in the idea of having kids...and in me too."

Terri reported that she is a paralegal for a major law firm in the city. She reluctantly explained that her income actually exceeded that of some of the other junior attorney associates because, "The partners say I do better research into their cases than they can do. Anybody can sit in a law library and look things up. It's no big deal really. They are very kind to me."

Terri's frustration came out as she lamented, "I just can't seem to please Bob anymore. I do my best to cook healthy and appealing meals when I get home from work. Bob's doctor tells him that his cholesterol is too high. He complains that everything I cook tastes like sawdust. He's probably right."

Terri stated that she suspects that she may have some as yet undetected medical problem. "It seems like I'm tired all the time. I use Saturday to clean the house. Bob loves sports, and I like to see him relaxing while the games are on. Sometimes I wish he'd pitch in a little more around the house, but he does take care of the lawn in the summer." She wanly recounted, "As my mom used to say, 'Men may work from sun-to-sun, but women's work is never done.'"

She concluded our initial session by thanking me for listening to her, adding "I hope you can show me how to be a better wife and make my husband happy."

***

In 1946, Dr. Benjamin Spock wrote the landmark pediatric text for parents, *Baby and Child Care*. Because of its usefulness to parents tending to their children's medical needs, it became a hugely popular layman's resource for addressing a multitude of daily maladies, injuries, and symptoms. Combining his expertise as a physician with his studies in psychoanalysis, Dr. Spock also made some observations regarding child psychology and parenting and expressed the view of the importance of children "feeling good about themselves." Thanks to the remarks of a pediatrician who had ventured into the arena of psychology, the self-esteem movement for children was born.

Dr. Spock's influence was enormous. He once mused that if he had known how popular his book would be become, he would have cautioned his editor that he was not a psychologist. His book's influence, nevertheless, has been most profound. The importance of children possessing a strong sense of self has permeated the education community and become part of our daily lexicon. It has defined and determined parenting techniques, our notion of boundaries for children and teens, and therefore affected how anyone under the age of sixty is likely to see himself/herself.

In the early stages of the twenty-first century, there are as many critics of the self-esteem movement as there are lingering supporters. Dr. Martin Seligman, in his book *The Optimistic Child* suggests that self-esteem is a function of achievement — that ultimately, the concept of giving someone a positive sense of self is a misnomer. Seligman tells us that we feel good about ourselves when we accomplish some goal.

Whether the reader sides more with Spock than Seligman or vice versa, today's women live within a cultural environment that focuses on self-esteem and influences their relationship choices. The concept of *homeostasis* suggests that we naturally seek balance in our lives. It is similar to the concept of a self-fulfilling prophecy. For example, an individual who is qualified for a new job she is seeking but who presents herself as uncertain of her abilities or qualifications is less likely to be selected than her similarly qualified counterpart who presents herself in a more confident manner. When the first applicant receives the inevitable rejection letter or phone call, she is disappointed but not surprised. Her diminished sense of self (an inward perception) leads to an external negative outcome. In a sad and unnecessary way, she has maintained a homeostatic condition. Her failure reinforces her negative sense of self. There is a regrettable balance between her limited sense of self and her failure to obtain the job she desired. On the other hand, the more optimistic applicant's achieving of her goal is a similar example of balance on the positive end of the homeostatic barometer.

In an attempt to enliven a session, I will sometimes ask clients, "Tell me everything you know about belly buttons." After getting over such an odd question, eventually we arrive at the notion that there are two kinds: *innies* and *outies*. I then explain that I like to think of all of us as fitting into one of those two categories *innies* or outies. In my admittedly fractured metaphor, *innies* are individuals who account for failure or disappointment by looking inward. They *do guilt* in the way that negatively addicted individuals do drugs. They are responsible women, certainly, but perhaps overly so. *Outies*, to complete the metaphor, see life's unsatisfying situations as caused by outside forces. *Outies* tend to blame others for their circumstances. *Outies* are frustrated by their situations and often correctly point out the shortcomings or abuses of others, but they fail to focus on the steps or strategies available to them to rectify or improve their plight.

Building on the theory of Julian Rotter, Bernard Weiner amplifies the concept of *locus of control* by explaining the same concept in less anatomical terms. He suggests that all of us view life through one of two points of view or *lenses*. Those with what he calls an *internal locus of control* are similar to *innies*. They tend to see their life outcomes, both successes and failures, as a result of either their own personal abilities (or weaknesses) or the product of their own effort (or lack thereof). Conversely, *outies* manifest what Weiner terms an *external locus of control*. They account for their positive and negative outcomes as flowing from very different sources or causes. *Outies* see life's vagaries as a reflection of either luck or the difficulty of the task itself. Winning or losing in a given environment is the result of *being lucky or unlucky*. Or they see defeat as being a result of an impossible situation or a win that anyone could have attained. *Outies* see themselves, metaphorically, as a bit of human flotsam adrift on an ocean of influence and chance that they can no more control than a leaf can steer itself in a blustery, autumn wind.

For women who appear to have found themselves in unsatisfying relationships due to a lack of their own positive self-regard, the preceding concepts and theories are very relevant. Later in this book, we will discuss steps that a woman can take to extricate herself from a poor pattern of relationship choice. For now, let's examine and review this pattern through the experience of our introductory hypothetical client, Terri.

In Terri, we see several clues into how and why she finds herself in an unhappy relationship situation. First of all, Terri is clearly an innie. She holds herself accountable for most, if not all, of the problems within her marriage, even while it is evident that she should not be doing so. She sees herself as a poor cook and an unappealing romantic partner. She discounts her achievements as a working professional woman and downplays the positive regard that her employers appear to have for her. She readily accepts a rather downtrodden view of the role and fate of women in general. Perhaps most pathetically, she expresses herself as having the singular responsibility to "make my husband happy." Clearly, one's happiness is, or should be, a matter of individual choice and responsibility. As the scenario of Terri implies, her assumption of the responsibility for all outcomes in her marriage conveniently allows her husband Bob to absent himself from any role in the creation and maintenance of their marital happiness.

How did Terri arrive at her negative perception of herself? Critical parents? An earlier failed relationship? A painful adolescent experience in middle school or high school with peers? It is less important to learn the answer to the "why" question than to explore what she can do to correct the situation. To begin, Terri and the readers of this book need to recognize their patterns of behavior. I tell my graduate students that all professional helpers—be they counselors, psychologists, or social workers—are not advisors. We are, instead, therapeutic *cabdrivers* or "professional mirror holders." Once a passenger enters the cabbie's vehicle, he does not tell the rider that she should go to the movie or the museum. The cabbie asks where the client wishes to go, and his expertise is in knowing the best path or strategy in order to arrive at that destination. Similarly, the professional mirror holder, by adjusting the metaphorical looking glass to different angles and positions, allows the client to perceive herself more clearly.

It is essential that Terri come to recognize her *innie* tendencies if she is going to establish more assertive future relationships. Ironically, this will serve not only her, but also her present or future partners. The woman who judges herself too harshly also inadvertently enables her partner to engage in a pattern of blaming and excuse-making. Ultimately, men with these tendencies are not successful in most areas of their life, even if they have found a woman who will tolerate their indolence. Perhaps even more importantly, women who allow themselves to be mistreated are unintentionally serving as terrible role models for their daughters as well as their sons. No mother wishes her daughter to be abused, nor does she want her sons to become abusers. It is perhaps a sad commentary on the value system of women who lack self-esteem that this point resonates with them more urgently than does the notion that they should not allow themselves to be abused.

The feminist psychologist, Carol Gilligan, tells us that most women value their children and their partners more than they value themselves. "My kids' needs (and my partner's) come before mine." Our culture also reviles women who put their own desires before those of their family members. Gilligan suggests that women need to take a more balanced approach to their lives and their resulting value system. She proposes that women should care for others, but also themselves to the same degree. Simply stated, women (especially those who are prone to a diminished sense of self) need to internally exclaim, "I count too!" Not more than, but in addition to, those they traditionally care for.

In summary, what are the key signs of a woman who is prone to making ill-advised relationship choices based upon *low self-esteem*? Let's list a few:

1   an exaggerated and misguided degree of responsibility for all and everything

2   a reluctance to accept credit or praise for achievements and accolades they have justly earned

3   a personal, past history of either abuse or parental neglect or diminishment

Women who have identified themselves as making poor relationship choices because of their lack of self-esteem tend to respond "true" to the following true-false queries:

• Faced with some failure or unsuccessful situation, I'm more likely to blame myself than to blame others.

• My friends and family will often say something like, "You're too hard on yourself."

- I tend to discount or reject compliments.

- Personal failures and disappointments are painful but not surprising.

- I have a negative opinion of my appearance. (Ed. Note: Most women report some degree of dissatisfaction with their appearance, i.e. height, weight, etc., but "Strand #1 women have an exaggerated negative view of themselves in this area.)

Statistical Highlights About Low Self-Esteem Females

As I mentioned in the introduction of this book, this data is based upon the survey responses of over 300 women that addressed their relationship choices. Due to incomplete responses on some of the surveys, the actual number of surveys used for data generation was 259. This data was collected from a broad spectrum of the female population, from teens to women in their sixties. All respondents were volunteers and were self-selected based upon their view of their past unsatisfying relationship experience. They completed the survey on their own time, individually, and returned the survey at their own pace and by their own choice. Listed below are some of the statistics drawn from their input:

- Fifty-nine percent of those surveyed identified *low self-esteem* as one of the factors leading to their choice of a partner.

- Thirty-six percent of those surveyed listed *low self-esteem* as the most important factor in their choice of a partner.

nurturing

Never allow someone to be your priority while
allowing yourself to be their option.

—Gabrielita

He's not a diaper; you can't change him!

—A. Jordan

Case Study: *Naiah*

Naiah was one of the brightest students in a graduate
course I taught in lifespan psychology. She was an elemen-
tary public school teacher working for the Detroit Public

School District for the past five years. Naiah had graduated from Cass Tech High School, probably the highest
rated magnet school of the Detroit school system at that
time. She had received scholarships to attend Eastern
Michigan University based upon both her excellent academic record and her financial need. She was comfortable
with the other students and quickly emerged as one of the
more verbal and expressive contributors. Her perspective
was helpful to the class in general.

About halfway through the course, Naiah came to
class in a more subdued mode than had been the case
during our first weeks. During our break time I asked
Naiah if there were something bothering her. She initially
demurred, but after a few moments of silently looking
away, she stated, "It's man trouble." She accepted my offer
to talk privately after class.

"Reggie and I have been living together for about fif-
teen months. I met him at a party at my cousin's house.
He told me that he was a college student at the time but
later admitted that he had only attended for part of one
semester a few years ago. He explained that he had to drop
out in order to work at the car wash to help his family. I
felt sorry for him. He seemed so sincere, and I offered to
help him go back to school." Eventually, Reggie moved
out after he met another woman at the community college course that Naiah had financed.

Naiah reported that while Reggie was her first live-in,
although she had had serious relationships in the past as
early as high school. She recounted that her first boyfriend,
Michael, was a special education student who depended
upon her, both emotionally and financially. "I helped him
study for his GED." She explained that Michael was nineteen at the time. "He always seemed as though he was so

close to getting it together back then." He talked about how much he appreciated me and loved me. He also would always tell me how beautiful I was although, as you can see, I'm not even close to being pretty." Naiah described how proud she was of the fact that Michael did eventually obtain his GED. She organized a graduation celebration for him, doing so on the weekend which was originally scheduled for her attendance at her own high school reunion. When questioned about her change of plans, Naiah smilingly explained, "There will be other reunions, but celebrating Michael's achievement was much more important." She conceded that her feelings were hurt when Michael broke up with her but, strangely, her upset was directed more at Michael's new girlfriend than Michael himself. Typically, Naiah would recite homilies such as, "It just didn't work out," or "I guess I just wasn't what Michael needed." At one work-related gathering, however, Naiah was heard to proclaim (after perhaps a few too many glasses of merlot), "Michael's new girlfriend will never take care of him the way I used to."

Since her breakup with Reggie, Naiah has been dating the father of two of her students. The father's wife divorced him as the result of a criminal conviction he received which led to thirty months of incarceration. He is in the process of "putting his life back together," according to Naiah. To that end, she recently loaned the student's father thirty thousand dollars for a down payment on a house in her school district and co-signed on the mortgage. She concluded, "If I don't help him get started, who will?"

———————————————

Both sociologists and anthropologists would tend to agree that women are natural nurturers. John Grey, in his immensely popular *Men Are from Mars and*

Women Are from Venus, characterizes women as being genetically hot-wired to focus on detail and care-giving activities while men are the ancestral hunter-gatherers whose vision tends to be broader in emphasis, surveying the landscape for threat and opportunity.

While our more technically-oriented culture does not necessarily revere stereotypically aggressive masculine behavior, we do not reject it either. For example, the common phrase "too much testosterone" has a typically ambiguous connotation. To make the point, what is the opposite of testosterone-driven behavior? Sensitive? Tender? Wimpy? How many men would be comfortable being described with those adjectives?

Conversely, there appears to be near universal respect and acknowledgement for what Grey would term "Venus-like" qualities for women. Characterizing a woman as a natural care-giver is surely seen as close to the top of any list of positive feminine qualities. As alluded to in the last chapter with reference to Carol Gilligan's work, we also see that women who manifest the stereotypical male qualities of aggression and dominance are seen as undesirable or unfeminine.

Simply stated, both men and women agree that the female as nurturer is a favorable and desirable assignation. How, then, can this positive trait be the single most common reason cited by women in my research as the cause for their past disastrous relationship choices?

First, consider some data based upon my research and survey of women who self-identify as individuals who found themselves in unsatisfying relationships. This book is essentially a representation of the responses provided by 259 women to a survey I developed (Appendix A). Those surveys revealed that the most common explanation for a woman's ill-advised relationship decision was based upon her desire to provide support or nurturing for her partner.

Once again, how can that be a bad thing? Isn't that what a relationship or marriage is supposed to be about? Obviously, the answer must be yes, but there are some qualifiers to that assumption.

Family systems theorists and practitioners describe the roles that children who grow up in dysfunctional families typically adopt. One of these roles is referred to as the *hero*. Hero children are those individuals who cope with their family's instability and chaos by trying to keep everything perfect. Whether they are assisting a mother in dealing with their father's drinking problem, or assisting a father in dealing with his wife's mental illness, the *hero* child derives earned gratification from the role as a helper to the co-dependent parent. While quietly sad about their negative family circumstances, heroes come to value the praise and appreciation they receive as helpers and supporters of their victimized parent and siblings. Heroes are often the oldest sibling in the family structure, or they function as though they were.

Sadly, their efforts are doomed to failure, because the source of the family's unhappiness cannot be solved by keeping the home neat or by having dinner on the table when the negatively addicted parent returns home. The *hero* carries her frustration forward as her best efforts seem to fail. Since she is a caregiver by choice (and probably by the modeling provided by a co-dependent parent), her way of addressing this failure is to simply try harder or to self deprecate, in the style of an *innie*. (See Chapter 1.)

Let's go back to Naiah to examine what clues exist to her assumed role as a nurturer. First of all, she acknowledges that her past relationships have invariably been with boys and men who did not match either her achievement or ambition. This is arguably the central characteristic for all of the six strands, but the clue to the fact that the woman (in this case, Naiah) is a nurturer is found in her response to the situation. In the previous chapter addressing low self-esteem, Terri basically accepted her partner's low level of achievement as a reflection of her own unworthiness. In other words, Terri's view may have been, "He's not so great, but neither am I." *Acceptance* may be a key descriptor of her response to an underachieving partner.

In Naiah's case, her partner's poor performance appears to be more motivating to action rather than simple acceptance of personal unworthiness. It is clear that Naiah sees herself as being responsible for doing something about the situation of her mate's lack of personal success. It should be noted that responsibility and blame are not synonymous concepts. Naiah almost certainly did not see herself as the cause for her boyfriend's past shortcomings. She would surely see the cause as something outside her. Nevertheless, she feels responsible for doing something to ameliorate the situation. For example, if we come upon a traffic accident while driving down a highway, we realize that we did not cause that accident. Most good citizens would still feel obligated to do something about the situation, however. We may stop and offer assistance or call 911 to report the incident. Most of us would not be comfortable simply driving past the scene without addressing it in some manner.

On the surface, therefore, Naiah is simply demonstrating her humanity and compassion by helping her succession of partners. This is where the difference between the Good Samaritan on the highway and the nurturing female partner becomes evident. The difference is perhaps best outlined by drawing a distinction between *helping* and *enabling*. The driver who stops at the accident site or calls for assistance is helping; the enabling support of the *nurturer* actually gets in the way of her partner's personal growth. Like a parent who completes her child's homework or does all the design and construction for a child's social studies project, the supportive (nurturing) partner is actually preventing or inhibiting her partner's growth by denying him-her a learning experience. A father who shows his son how to hit a baseball by demonstrating a series of line drives in a batting cage is doing little to develop his son or daughter's hand-eye coordination. He may provide a visual illustration with one or two swings, but then should allow the child to learn by donning the helmet and making his-her own hits and misses.

Nurturers never seem to fully grasp this concept. Intellectually, they may understand the notion of enabling, but emotionally, they appear unable to resist the desire to intervene. Nurturers proceed from a sort of "one last time" thinking. In other words, while they seem to understand that their partner is unlikely to grow without making some *bad swings* at the fastballs of life, the inclination to rescue "one last time" is too powerful to resist. So they pay one more overdue bill of their partner, write one more paper for their procrastinating student-husband, or call an employer with another bogus story to rescue their hung-over mate. When (big surprise!) the latest partner bailout fails to lead to any greater level of responsible behavior, the nurturers remain frustrated and disappointed. Even worse, they are frustrated by their own inability to terminate the behavior (their own) that keeps their partner indolent and unsuccessful.

Perhaps the cruelest reality for the nurturer may be summarized with this idea:

> The beggar hates his benefactor.

Sadly, this appears to juxtapose the logical course and outcome of the charitable act. Imagine that an individual passes a beggar in the street and throws coins in the hat of the supplicant. The patron may feel sorry for the plight of the beggar and may be gratified by his-her own act of charity. The giver may assume that the beggar appreciates and even admires his benefactor. Ironically, it is likely that the receiver begrudges the giver's failure to provide a more substantial gratuity. If the giver provides a five dollar bill, the supplicant may resent not being proffered a twenty.

We may characterize the beggar as an *outie* who chooses to direct personal disappointments and frustrations on others, and this is a proper analysis. Regrettably, the *outie* underachiever has found a soul-mate in the nurturer. Just as he is unwilling to accept responsibility for his lack of accomplishment, his nurturer-partner seems to desperately don the mantle of responsibility for assisting his-her partner. If guilt becomes part of this unhealthy and non-productive *dance,* it is the nurturer who bears it rather than her blaming and complaining partner.

It can be said that every relationship is like a dance. Imagine that you are attending a wedding with your partner. As you sit near the edge of the dance floor, the two of you observe a couple floating effortlessly across the floor. Clearly, they are an experienced pair, and they are enjoying their talent. Your mate comments, "Aren't those two impressive? They're movements are identical!"

Strictly speaking, their steps are not identical, but rather, complementary. As the male dancer slides to his left, his partner is gliding to her right, not her left. If he is moving forward, she is backing up. And so on. As we apply the analogy to other relationships, we recognize the principle of complementary action. In an abusive relationship, for example, one partner berates or physically menaces the other while the passive member of the couple simply takes the abuse. One husband or boyfriend is dancing to the beat of anger while his wife or girlfriend responds to the tune of sadness and guilt. It is a dysfunctional, symbiotic relationship. Regrettably, both members of the twosome are trapped in a pattern of painful and self-defeating action and reaction. And the pattern continues, with the music of the dance becoming louder and more compelling as the dancers repeat their patterned steps with increasing pace and destructive rhythms.

And as any professional who works with the victims can attest, there is one universal principle regarding abusive conduct: *it is progressive!* Abuse may escalate from verbal castigation to physical intimidation. It may advance from sarcastic criticism to profane denigration.

Going back to our unhappy teacher, Naiah, some striking patterns emerge. First, we see a string of relationships with men that follow a similar path. The two prior relationships (with Michael and Reggie) both ended when the men left her. The break-up occurred after Naiah had invested a great deal of time (and money) in the two involvements. Strangely, while Naiah tends to gloss over the role that the men themselves appeared to play in the dissolution of the relationship, she is subtly critical of the men's future partners. While Naiah is an apparently high-achieving person in her own professional life, she also appears to manifest outie tendencies with regard to her relationships. Instead of looking at her actions that may be generating guilty feelings within her partners, Naiah looks outside herself for reasons for her past break-ups, such as her former mates' next female partners.

Despite her two past unsuccessful outcomes, Naiah appears to be jumping back into the metaphorical frying pan that singed her in the past. She is lending money to the father of her two students. Is she trying to be genuinely helpful? Almost certainly. Is Naiah a good-hearted woman? Once again, clearly so. But she is repeating a failed pattern that seeks, in addition to her genuine altruism, to curry appreciation as well. She fails to comprehend that, ultimately, the men in her life resent her indulgence. While they accept her assistance, they also are bothered by it.

It is the difference between being a supportive partner and enabling. Until she grasps that concept, until she is able to look critically into the introspective mirror to perceive the impact of the pattern she has created, her disappointments will invariably continue.

You are a *nurturer* if:

- you continue to *help* even when you don't feel good about doing so, on some level.

- you continue to help, even when the partner continues *not* to change or improve.

- you see your behavior as that of a typical hero from a dysfunctional family.

- you find yourself strangely disinterested in more functional potential partners.

- you are clearly working harder at the relationship than your partner.

excitement

I was nauseous and tingly all over. I was
either in love or had the smallpox.

—Woody Allen

Case Study: *Allison*

Allison was a young woman in her mid-thirties who was
in the early stages of her master's program in counseling
at Michigan State University. She had graduated from a
small, prestigious private college remarking, "I know that
I got in based on my high SAT (college entrance exam)
score. It couldn't have been based upon my high school
grade-point average; that sucked." She explained that she

was currently employed in an art gallery and was also a sculptor herself. She was seeking a counseling degree in the hope that she could become a practitioner of art therapy. She explained that she had spent time studying eastern philosophy, adding "I think that the West understands left brain stuff well in terms of what works in counseling, but there is a need to incorporate more right-brain thinking into how we counsel people."

I must admit to a fairly high degree of generationally triggered bias against Allison initially. She was vividly and vibrantly colored with tattoos which covered portions of her exposed arms and neck area. As the semesters unfolded, however, she demonstrated both a high degree of academic competence as well as an insightful mind in discussing hypothetical clients and cases. Her opinions and strategies with clients were well-drawn, and she showed no reluctance to perform in front of her more reticent classmates during mock fishbowl counseling sessions which were critiqued by both professor and peers alike. Her academic progress was not the reason for her request for an appointment during my office hours, however.

"Dr. Farrar, why am I a loser magnet?" Allison then recounted a series of failed or unsatisfying relationships that seemed to follow a similar pattern. "Going back as far as ninth grade, I always seemed to be drawn to the wrong guys. My first boyfriend was a senior who got kicked out of school for selling drugs. I didn't really like that he sold, but he introduced me to pot, and I admit that I liked it."

Allison then went on to describe similar boyfriends, some older or, by eleventh grade, in her own class. She reflected, "I always was in advanced classes, but none of my boyfriends were. I felt good about my looks, although sometimes my women teachers would say things like,

'Allison, why do you dress like a biker when you're such a pretty girl?' A couple times, a few of the jocks or nerds would ask me out, but I wasn't really interested. One was really cute, but he was such a straight arrow that he turned me off. I didn't think I'd have any fun with him."

She stated that her first sexual experience took place near the end of ninth grade with her first high-school boyfriend. "It probably wasn't the smartest thing I ever did. We didn't have any protection, and I knew he'd been with other pretty-sleazy girls. But I always wanted to know what it (sex) would be like." Allison later confided that she had contracted a venereal disease which, fortunately, had been successfully treated.

"I've made bad choices before, Doc, but I'm no dummy, as you know. What's going on with me that I can't seem to get into nice guys?"

Over my thirty years of professional experience in treating addictions, I have encountered several theoretical models that seek to account for self destructive patterns involving addictions. Some focus on genetic predisposition, some on socio-cultural elements. One of the theories that may have applications for Allison (and other women who seem to be drawn to the "bad boys" of their culture) revolves around the hormone adrenalin. The so called adrenalin theory suggests that all human beings can be plotted somewhere on a continuum with risk-taking (or adrenalin-seeking) behavior at one end and security-oriented (or adrenalin-aversive) behavior at the other. This theory suggests that some of us naturally seek stimulation while others of us find that same sensation to be annoying or discomforting in some way.

During the course of a routine, physical examination some years ago, my physician and I had a discussion surrounding two recent court-mandated evaluations I had conducted on adjudicated defendants. The first evaluation involved an individual who was literally on his way to federal prison due to his involvement in drug trafficking. He candidly acknowledged that he had an extensive drug history, engaging in the use of virtually every form of recreational as well as prescription drugs. When questioned about his experience with cocaine, the respondent acknowledged that he had experimented with it and had, in fact, employed it as a tool to keep him awake during marathon driving trips to southern Florida to pick up and deliver drugs as a so-called mule. He explained, "I'd drive from Detroit to Miami non-stop, pick up a shipment, and turn around to return to Detroit, also non-stop. I'd use cocaine to stay awake and, of course, I was paranoid the whole time for fear of getting busted. I'd go the speed limit and drive a non-descript car." Ironically, the future convict observed, "I never really liked cocaine. I never got that great high from it. To me, it was like drinking twenty cups of coffee. It just made me jittery. But I liked that it kept me awake for those long drives to Miami. Personally, I always preferred heroin."

The second client I had interviewed, coincidentally the same day as the above client, also admitted to a broad history of substance involvement. When questioned about his view of cocaine, his response was strikingly different than the previous client. Looking almost wistfully into the distance, apparently recalling past use of that stimulant, he shared, "You know, Doc, I've tried everything, but there's nothing like cocaine. People say that it's better than sex, and they are right. Or sex is best with cocaine. There's nothing like it."

I shared these two interviews with my physician and asked him if he could account for such a marked difference from two cocaine users who were describing disparate reactions from what was, presumably, the same substance. He offered, "It may come down to individual physiological differences between the two men. Each of us has what might be considered our optimum pleasure zone." At this point, the doctor raised his hand above his head, suggesting a high level. He explained, "Some of us have a high threshold for pleasure and, therefore, prefer stimulating substances and experiences." He then lowered his hand to waist level and continued, "Some of us find stimulants to be aversive or annoying. Those individuals prefer some placid, sedate experiences. Such people would lean toward more relaxing, soothing experiences. Their optimum pleasure experience would be lower, if you will. Your two clients might have varied in this way. The man you described as the drug mule preferred heroin because his optimum pleasure zone was lower. Cocaine simply bothered him, although he used its stimulating effects to keep him awake. The second client had a higher pleasure zone and found that cocaine hit his spot."

I thought about my doctor's observations about other experiences individuals have that may reflect such differences between people. While most of us enjoy a back rub, for example, some of us welcome a vigorous kneading of our muscles while others prefer a mink-glove, soothing experience. When attending an amusement park, the adrenalin seekers head straight for the roller coasters while the adrenalin-aversive patrons amble toward a merry-go-round or even a park bench. Those into *excitement* will pay three figures to jump out of an airplane as a skydiver while risk-aversive people would pay the same sum in order to be excused from such a risky exercise.

Looking back into my work with Allison, the issue of adrenalin-seeking behavior theory may have some resonance. She candidly acknowledged that she had always been drawn to high-risk behaviors and men alike. On a cognitive level, while she appreciated and recognized the values and accomplishments of her studious male peers, she also conceded that she found them "kinda boring. They're nice guys, but..."

My experience is the "nice guys, but..." phenomenon typifies the response of the woman who fits the *excitement* strand. Women who fit the profile of the *excitement* strand are both bad-boy seekers and magnets. As I recall my doctor holding his measured right hand above his head to reflect a high capacity for stimulation, I can see how this is descriptive of the stance such women have in their mate selection. Like the skydiver (or even the compulsive gambler), the *excitement* a woman gets from a risky relationship is more important than the inevitably negative, often disastrous outcome.

Any animal trainer knows that a given behavior can be best ingrained through the principle of intermittent reinforcement. This means that, in order for a given behavior to continue, the trainer *does not* provide the reward (i.e. a fish for Shamu or a dog biscuit for Fido) after every appropriate behavioral response. Instead, the reward is introduced on occasional, unpredictable intervals. Ironically, the desired behavior continues longer under this pattern. The dog or the dolphin never knows if the treat is coming or not. If he has been trained to receive a reward after every occurrence, the behavior is terminated (extinguished) rather quickly if the reinforcement is removed. The animal learns that the reward is no longer forthcoming. It knows the game is over rather quickly. If the reinforcer had been intermittent in nature, it will take the animal longer to give up on the behavior that earlier generated the reward. Intermittent reinforcement is more effective than constant reinforcement.

How animals are trained may (or may not) be interesting to us, but what does that have to do with women and their choice of mates? How is this relevant to Allison? Let's eavesdrop into this hypothetical conversation between two women who we will refer to Anna and Bella.

Anna	How was your date with Wally last night?
Bella	It was fine, I guess. He took me out for dinner, let me pick the movie we went to afterward, and sent me flowers this morning.
Anna	Sounds great. What do you think?
Bella	I don't know. Wally's a nice guy, but…
Anna	Hmm. Well, if you heard from Rocky? I know you had that date with him a couple of weeks ago.
Bella	Yeah, that was quite an experience. He picked me up on his motorcycle. My hair got all blown around. We went to this bar, and guess what? He didn't have enough money for the bill, so I had to pick up the check. He said he'd call, but I haven't heard from him yet.
Anna	Good riddance.
Bella	Yeah, I guess. Still, I kinda wish I'd hear from him.

Imagine that there is a young man, Jason, listening into the conversation of the two girls from an adjacent table. As the conversation unfolded, he might assume that Bella would be taken by the generous and attentive behaviors of Wally. Why? Because Wally exhibited all the behaviors that women state that they appreciate. He was generous, respectful, and followed up with attention (flowers) after their date. Jason would probably be surprised by Bella's indifference to Wally's attentions. He would also likely be surprised by Bella's desire to hear from Rocky, even though he demonstrated an apparent lack of consideration and attentiveness both during and after their date.

As portrayed, Rocky is probably an unlikely psychology major, but he also exhibits an intuitive understanding of the principle of intermittent reinforcement. We might refer to this as the *keep 'em guessing* approach. Bella remains interested in Rocky, in part, because she is never quite sure when (or if) he is going to call. When she may be close to giving up on him, he will call her, once again raising her interest and hopes. Conversely, if Wally says he will call the next day, he invariably does so. He is predictable. He isn't exciting. For the Bellas of the world, this is not enough stimulation or adrenalin for them.

You may be an *excitement* woman if:

- conventional activities, modes of dress, and lifestyles are uninteresting or dull to you.

- you are easily bored or have trouble paying attention to routine activities and events.

- you have a tattoo or piercings (or several), wish you had one, or look favorably on those who do.

- if you have a *conventional* job (i.e., teacher, minister, accountant) or family life, you welcome opportunities to *break out* when the situation makes such changes possible.

- you enjoy risky pastimes such as motorcycling, skydiving, scuba, or gambling.

> In real love, you want the other person's good. In romantic love, you want the other person.
>
> —Margaret Anderson

control

There are two things over which you have complete dominion authority and control: your mind and your mouth.

—African Proverb

Case Study: *Kathleen*

Kathleen was referred to me by a former colleague who had taken a job at an inpatient, substance-abuse facility after she left the outpatient clinics I had previously administered. Kathleen was the wife of an alcoholic who had recently completed a four-week inpatient stay to address his thirty-year-history of heavy drinking. Her husband's family therapist from the residential facility recommended outpatient counseling to help her address issues she will be facing as her husband's recovery evolved.

Kathleen was a woman who appeared to be in her late forties or early fifties. She was of average height and perhaps slightly overweight. She arrived wearing a gray, business suit and announced that she had taken two hours off from her job as the office manager of a local construction company to attend the appointment. She wearily reported that she had despaired of her husband ever quitting his drinking, instead moving forward in his life "for the sake of our three children." When her husband lost his job as a union electrician due to his unreliable attendance at various work sites, Kathleen responded to a want-ad that sought a clerical support person at her current company. She proudly explained, "Once I got there, it was apparent that the office needed a lot more organization and structure. When the former office manager left, I was offered the position by the owners. They said they needed someone who wasn't just everyone's friend."

Kathleen then related a long history of frustration with her husband Charley's drinking. "No matter what I did, he would find a way to get alcohol. First it was beer. Later it turned into vodka. I'd count his drinks at first. I'd also have to remind him to cut back in social situations. It got to the point where I'd be searching his workroom and dresser drawers for bottles."

Although Kathleen lamented her situation, she stated that the family was less adversely affected by Charley's drinking because of her disciplined approach to the family's business. "Ironically, I think my husband's drinking actually helped me find myself. Of course, I wish his drinking problem wasn't so bad, but I feel good about keeping the family together." She explained that she had developed a bill-paying system that was based upon the one she developed at work. "I have a *tickler system* that comes up on my home computer, so I know when a bill is due. That way I don't pay them too early. A day of interest on your own money is a day of interest earned."

She then stated that, although she appreciated the concern of the counselors at the treatment center, she had trouble understanding why she had been referred for counseling. "My husband is the one who needs to get his act together, not me."

A question often posed in family therapy that bewilders, then irritates, the wives of men in treatment for their alcohol problem is, "What is the payoff for having an alcoholic husband?" Not surprisingly, those wives often retort that there is no benefit for such a painful situation. Their lives have been ruined because of their spouses' failure to control their drinking. Curiously, often these women challenge the word alcoholic when it is applied to their partners. Instead, they observe something like, "He's not an alcoholic; he just doesn't manage his drinking all the time. If he'd just show some self-control, we wouldn't be in this situation."

But back to the original question: What is the payoff to having an alcoholic (or compulsive gambler, or a man who isn't able to hold a job) husband or partner? The answer, simply stated, is that she is able to be the boss. While we stereotypically refer to women as the weaker sex, physical dominance or superiority plays a limited role in a civilized society, at least in non-physically abusive households. To paraphrase the time-honored maxim, "The pen is mightier than the sword." In most relationships the more apt bromide might be, "The word wields more power than the fist."

Most of us would tend to define verbal abuse in masculine terms or behavior patterns. In other words, we tend to picture a verbally abusive person as being overtly insulting or deprecating in tone and choice of verbiage. Name-calling, threats of violence, and observations that cut to the heart of an individual's self-esteem are what most of us imagine when we consider language to be verbally abusive. And, of course, all of those forms of dialogue are, in fact, very abusive. They also fit the image of typically male forms of aggression.

Perhaps we can picture Marlon Brando as Stanley Kowalski from *Streetcar Named Desire* menacing Blanche. Or we envision Carlo, from *The Godfather*, insulting and eventually beating his wife, Connie, who was the Godfather's daughter. (Bad move, Carlo!). These are vivid images that define our view of both physical and verbal abuse. It is much harder to think of pictures or examples of women engaging in like conduct with a cowering husband or boyfriend. The most obvious explanation for this difficulty is that most females don't act this way.

Well, how do they demonstrate verbal abuse (which seems to correlate with control-oriented behavior)? It appears that women manifest verbal abuse through more subtle, but persistent jabs and digs. If men can verbally guillotine their partners with profanity-strewn epithets, women can maintain control over their diminished mates with the Chinese metaphor of a "thousand small cuts."

Because of its subtlety, this pattern of dialogue is more easily defended or rationalized. While only the most boorish of men could defend a four-letter word diatribe or expressed intention to maim or disfigure, most women can probably defend controlling the family finances by explaining, "You know how he gets if he has a few extra dollars to play poker with." This presumed decision of incompetence by her husband might, at best, generate a few knowing nods from her family members or chuckles from her girlfriends during a coffee break. No one would accuse the usurper of the family checkbook to be abusive. In fact, such behavior is more likely to elicit sympathy than a rebuke. Kathleen (from above) is more likely to hear a compassionate "That's all you need, my dear, another job monitoring him," than the insightful query, "How do you think he feels when you make a remark about money and poker in front of his children or his family?"

The payoff for having a diminished partner is *control*. While this strand in our research does not appear as frequently as low self-esteem or nurturing, the motivation and resulting pattern is as identifiable as the others. It is worthy of note that, in some ways, nurturing behavior and controlling behavior may appear similar, at least on the surface. Both involve *doing for* the male partner. The difference is that the nurturer is invariably helping in the hope that she can elevate her partner in some functional way, or at least assist him in avoiding making more mistakes or failures. For the *control* woman, the assisting behavior has the opposite goal (or at least the effect) of disabling the male partner. While the nurturer almost pathetically seeks to give to her partner at the expense of her own needs, the *control* woman's behaviors are self-centered rather than other-centered. While the nurturer demonstrates too much empathy, the controlling woman exhibits very little.

Individuals in white-collar environments understand that there are two ways to climb the corporate ladder.

One can either progress up the rungs at greater speed than one's colleagues, or can advance by pulling the others off the ladder. In the case of our control-strand women, they make themselves look better by having a weak or incompetent partner beside them. Like the other strands, this is almost certainly an unconscious, rather than pre-meditated, decision. The Kathleens of our study, like the others, don't apply introspective thought to their mate selection. They are caught in a pattern of power-seeking, but ultimately unrewarding conduct that mires them in a relationship (or series of relationships) with men that do not meet their emotional, financial, or intellectual needs. Or even worse, perhaps they do meet some other need that is dysfunctional and unhealthy.

How do the women who fit the control profile account for their ongoing disappointments with the men in their lives? In Chapter 1 we discussed the concept of locus of control. Control *outies* lament their circumstances but typically take no responsibility or ownership of them. Inside, they may tend to blame their partners for their problems and, of course, those partners gave them ample justification for the *outies'* blaming with their own non-productive behavior. It is yet another example of the dance metaphor that we described in Chapter 2. Just as the nurturer of chapter 2 has found a perfect partner in an emotionally needy male, the control seeking woman of Chapter 4 has unearthed her ideal mate in the person of a weak and ineffectual man.

At times in marriage counseling, I tell couples during a joint session of a seemingly irrational equation. I will suggest to Mr. X, "You control ninety to ninety-five percent of this relationship." I will take the same position with Mrs. X, also suggesting that she controls the same ninety to ninety-five percent of the outcomes within the marriage or partnership. Mathematically this, of course, does not compute. But I report in this fashion to make a point. I will continue, explaining, "Obviously, Mrs. X, you generate fifty percent of the communication in this relationship Additionally, in this very free country of ours, most of us have willingly chosen our partners. Arranged marriages are not the common method of partner determination in 21st century America. You chose Mr. X, and it may be useful for us to consider what motivated your choice of him." Naturally, I then turn to Mr. X and remind him that the same statistics and choices apply to him as well. In other words, each partner, through the choice of mate and as a result of communication and input, is largely the master and determiner of their world.

Some may accuse this author (and perhaps Dale Carnegie for some of his advice in *How to Win Friends and Influence People*) of advocating manipulative behavior. Whether that is true or not, I do believe that we are largely the masters of our relationship outcomes. For example, I have been married for over forty years to my lovely wife. I made the tactical error, on our first date, of expressing the observation, "I thought you would be more docile." Not a good move on my part. My wife is not docile but, fortunately for me and our future children at that time, she married me anyway.

My point is that my wife is not docile, and I have come to know, understand, and appreciate her dispositional nature. Armed with that knowledge, I have the ability to shape my dialogue accordingly. I realize, for example, that if I were to thunder into the kitchen from work one evening and exclaim, "I want my dinner now!" as I pounded my fist on the dinner table, I would be wearing her prepared linguini rather than dining on it. If I preferred the linguini as a repast rather than as an Italian chapeau, I would avoid that tone and that command. Knowing her as I do, a simple comment, "Boy, am I glad to be home. Dinner smells great." will yield a proud smile, a kiss, and a pleasant evening. Which do I want? A Neapolitan hairpiece or food and, perhaps, cuddles later? I pretty much know which remark is going to produce which outcome. I really do control my evening's destiny, almost all of the time. In like manner, my wife knows what works with me as well. Each of us, in a loving way, influences and largely controls the other by our actions and messages.

This counseling approach, hopefully, begins to move each client away from the common tendency of any relationship: blaming. It empowers each partner (both the controlling woman and her inept partner) to recognize that they have my metaphorical ninety-five percent control over the relationship. Ideally, it also allows the woman who is prone to seeking control to look at her own needs which are being sadly satisfied by her partner's dysfunction.

The noted psychologist and research expert in the field of marital stability, John Gottman, has done some fascinating laboratory studies on partner behavior. Dr. Gottman, through the use of videotaped sessions of marriage counseling, has identified specific physical and verbal behaviors that reflect a deteriorating marital relationship. Specifically, he speaks of his "Four Horsemen" of defensiveness, criticism, stonewalling, and contempt. But of the four, Gottman suggests that the most damaging is contempt. He explains that contempt implies a hierarchical stance; that the contemptuous partner is better than, or superior to, the contemptible mate. Describing one's partner as selfish or insensitive is critical behavior and certainly won't enhance a relationship, but calling your mate stupid or worthless is even more destructive. It involves looking down on the partner, and Gottman asserts that this conduct is even more damaging than criticism.

Certainly, the operative style and manner of the *controller* oozes a sense of superiority. Referring back to the dance metaphor, it may be very difficult for the *controller* to accept her partner if he, in fact, becomes more functional. The controller, consciously or unconsciously, is seeking higher ground. Instead of recognizing the benefit of having a more contributing and helpful partner, she may drive him away by not allowing him to grow. And if he does leave, the controller who lacks insight may go back to her old habit of blaming with, "After all I did for that man, and he leaves me as soon as he gets a job. What an ingrate."

And how resistant is our *controller* to looking in the mirror and recognizing her role in their old, sad dance?

You may be a *controller* if you:

- have a tendency to finish your partner's stories, or even sentences.

- narrate *amusing* stories about your partner's foibles or missteps.

- insist on making all important decisions or having the final word on all issues.

- constantly monitor the efforts and performance of the partner's tasks.

- outwork your partner and assume a martyr posture while reiterating your untiring efforts to support the spouse and family.

desire to be nurtured

You know what the trouble with real life
is? There's no danger music.

—Cable Guy

Case Study: *Maria*

Maria was a quiet eighteen-year-old attending her school district's alternative program. She was referred to counseling by her mother who explained, "She was a good girl and a good student before she met *that boy!* Since then, she's been skipping school, getting dropped from class for poor attendance, and failing because she doesn't turn in homework. When one of those clip things you use with marijuana fell out of her book bag one day, the principal suggested that she might do better at a different school."

Maria reported that she had lost interest in school around the time she met her boyfriend Jose. She explained, "I met him at the roller rink over the summer between ninth and tenth grade. He was so cute, and I was so taken with him right from the start. I couldn't believe it when he called me up for a date." Maria then recounted how attentive he was with her, right from the beginning. "He would say that he just wanted me all to himself. It felt great to have someone care about you so much."

Maria stated that she lived with her mother and older brother. Her parents divorced when she was ten, a result of her father's chronic, compulsive gambling. "When my dad does come by, he is always nice to me. He'll buy me something if he has money. Sometimes he does, but sometimes he borrows money. He never pays it back, but it's okay. He forgets. I just like to see him."

The young woman averted her eyes as she stammered through her report of a recent situation. "I don't know what happened with Jose. After a while, he started complaining about me spending time with my girlfriends. When I told him I'd promised to go to my friend's birthday party, for no reason, he slapped me." The next day, he brought me flowers and told me how sorry he was. I believed him. But it keeps getting worse. Now I fear him more than love him."

This fifth strand from my culling of female input was actually inspired by a visit I made to the employment of one of my graduate students, Ellen. Ellen was working at a residential facility for adjudicated youth. She was serving essentially as a house mother for her charges but also runs required daily group sessions with a co-therapist who was also a student of mine. Her girls ranged in age from thirteen to seventeen. The facility actually provided similar services for both males and females, although they were housed separately. The students attended the local high school during the day but lived at the facility for the remainder of the day and on weekends as well. Ellen explained that the average length of stay was about nine months with some girls remaining there up to fourteen months. The length of stay was determined by their progress through the program's stage format.

My original cataloging of my findings had yielded only five strands to explain the reporting women's choices of partner. At least, I thought so at the time. While Ellen had invited me to explain my theories about female mate selection to her girls, I came away with more new information than I probably had provided to my audience of nineteen girls.

I briefly went through the five strands identified so far (low self-esteem, nurturing, control, and *chemistry*. (Chemistry will be discussed in Chapter 6.) and explained them for the residents. I was actually more interested in hearing from the nineteen girls in attendance, however. The girls were surprisingly open about their personal backgrounds, including the behaviors that led to their juvenile justice program placements. At the time, I considered it to be a compliment to the talent of Ellen in engaging the residents and gaining their trust. As each girl's mini-biography was related, the stories began to follow a sadly predictable pattern. Their stories invariably included initial attraction to a boy or man, some involvement with alcohol and-or other drugs, sexual acting out (generally unprotected), and eventually some criminal activity. These offenses most commonly involved retail fraud (shoplifting), but many admitted being involved with drug dealing in concert with the former boyfriend. Two of the girls were pregnant and were to be transferred to another facility as their condition progressed. Ellen later confided (without breeching confidentiality by identifying the specific residents) that some of the girls were involved in prostituting themselves as well. This also appeared to occur via the *assistance* of their former boyfriends. I was not surprised that none of the girls chose to share that sad fact with me during my visit.

Interestingly, Ellen had earlier explained that she had actually worked previously in the boys' side of the residential unit. When I asked for some of her observations as to the differences in working with females versus males, she animatedly revealed, "The differences were enormous. The boys didn't want to be in the facility any more than the girls, and they fought a lot with each other. But boys didn't object to living with other guys per se. They appeared to be better able to resolve their grievances and move on. The girls invariably said that they didn't want to have to live with a bunch of females. They would lament that they preferred the company of males to females. One of our treatment goals is to help them to develop positive alliances with other girls."

Near the conclusion of my two-hour visit, Ellen helped me out by posing two very salient questions to the nineteen girls. She asked, "Without getting into blaming or excuse-making (Ellen had earlier explained privately that learning to accept responsibility was another major treatment goal), how many of you can honestly report that the behavior that led you to be in this facility had something to do with a relationship you were in at the time — a boyfriend, fiancé, etc.?" Nineteen hands were raised as the girls' heads were nodding in affirmation. Ellen then asked the second question that led to the birth of a new, sixth strand. She queried, "How many of you have an ongoing relationship with your biological father—letters, visits, regular phone calls?" One girl raised her hand. Later she privately explained that her father called her frequently and was very loving but also had a serious problem with alcohol.

After that most enlightening two-question sequence, I asked the girls to describe the boys-men that they were involved with prior to their arrests or adjudications. The girls generally described young men who were anywhere from two to ten years older than they. They related how flattered they were at the time that "An older guy was interested in me. My girlfriends thought it was cool too. I felt more mature."

At that point, many of Ellen's students began to sound very similar to Maria, our example from this chapter's introduction. They narrated whirlwind romances with the old boyfriend being attentive and complimentary. The phrase, (in various forms) "I was the best thing that ever happened to him." was expressed repeatedly. When the girls were introduced to unfamiliar, sexual activities or substance experimentation, they were sometimes coaxed into the behavior by being chided "not to act like a kid." More often, however, many girls conceded, "He never really had to talk me into anything. I wanted to please him, because he was so good to me." A pretty Hispanic girl ruefully reflected, "I don't know what I was thinking back then. Now it seems so obvious what he was doing." As I watched the girls while she spoke, several nodded in agreement while a few just looked down. One little blonde was shaking her head in apparent disagreement and blurted, "My boyfriend wasn't like that at all. He really loves me." Eye-rolling and exasperated looks ensued from the other girls in the meeting. The tall, thin girl sitting next to me tapped my knee and whispered, "She's a newbie."

As I left after thanking the girls for their help and input, Ellen shared a personal, final observation drawn from her experiences on both the boys' and the girls' wings of the facility. She reflected, "You know, Dr. Farrar, that I can't recall one of our boys in the other wing saying that he got into trouble because of some girl. No guy gets *led astray* by his girlfriend. But I can't think of a girl who wasn't negatively influenced by some guy. As you heard me explain before, we don't let the girls use that as a cop-out, but that does appear to be the prevailing pattern."

Thanks to Ellen's girls, the sixth strand was created. I labeled it a *desire to be nurtured*. While not exactly the polar opposite of its similar sounding predecessor, nurturing, it appears to stem from fairly specific backgrounds, demographics, and personality traits. Often, the girls and women who identify *desire to be nurtured* as their dominant motivation for their poor relationship choices are younger, at least in relation to their dysfunctional partners. They may not be as young as the students described earlier, but the notion that they are seeking a mentor, if not an outright father figure, routinely presents itself.

As alluded to earlier, these females reported an either absent or unsatisfactory male role model in their lives. The observation of many girls from the residential facility that no one coerced them into their ill-advised activities reminded me of some of my early days as a clinical director. In the 80s and 90s I ran a network of treatment and prevention programs in substance abuse which were geared to adolescents and young adults.

Typically teens would scoff at the idea that peer pressure played a part in their drug involvement. They would jibe, "No one forces a drink down our throat or a joint into our mouths. We do it because we want to." Looking back, those adolescents were being simultaneously truthful and incorrect. Whether they understood it or not, peer pressure was very much involved in their initial substance use. The pressure came from within them rather than from someone outside them, however. Nobody ever dragged them behind the gym and forced a joint between their lips. More often, the first time user willingly walked over to the group behind the school, asking, "What are you guys up to?" When invited to take a drag, the novice readily agreed. So much for earnest pledges made at DARE program commencements. In like fashion, the-desire-to-be-nurtured woman typically seeks out, or at least invites with her withering demeanor and thirst for approval and support, the male who, either systemically or unknowingly, is similarly after that type of woman. It is perhaps another example of the dance metaphor we described in Chapter 2. While a healthier woman (or perhaps a woman prone to the *excitement* or control strands) might be either suspicious or turned off by such premature or obsequious praise, the-desire-to-be-nurtured female revels in it. It is manna to a girl who is starving for male attention, affection, and approval.

In her best selling work on unhealthy relationships, *Men Who Hate Women and the Women Who Love Them*, Dr. Susan Forward bases the tenet of her work on the concept of misogyny. Simply put, misogynists hate women. These men may not realize their latent feelings but they, nevertheless, carry out their hatred and blaming behavior on their women. Certainly, Freudian psychology, with its emphasis on hidden motivation, has much to theorize about vis-á-vis this pattern of abuse. But Dr. Forward's work appears to present girls and women who fit into this book's category of desire to be natured.

In summary, those fitting the *desire to be nurtured* strand often are younger. Or at least, they tend to be naïve. One might also theorize or speculate that that there is an element of low self-esteem present as well. As mentioned earlier when we discussed the survey I used to gather my data for this work, most women self describe as a combination of at least two of my six strands.

You may be a *desire-to-be-nurtured* woman if:

- your partner is significantly older (relatively speaking) than you.

- your partner has far more experience than you in one or several life areas (i.e. sex, substance involvement, criminal activity)

- in retrospect, your relationship with your dysfunctional partner evolved (on his part) from one of attentiveness and support to control and ridicule.

- you had a distant or non-supportive relationship with your biological father or other significant adult male in your life.

chemistry

The ruling passion, be what it will.
The ruling passion conquers reason still.

—Alexander Pope

Case Study: *Jennifer*

I met Jennifer while attending a professional conference. She had recently earned her doctorate from a respected university. She was looking forward to assuming her first position as a member of her university's counseling center and also starting a part-time position as a contractual therapist at a local outpatient clinic. During the course of our conversation, she shared that she had some concerns about her recent marriage. She explained, "I knew my husband since high school. I don't know why, but I was always drawn to him. I was just comfortable with him. Honestly, we never really had anything in common. I was into books, and he was into sports and working with his hands. It was kind of cool being the girl of a football player. Football is everything down South, you know. But that wasn't it, either. Jake's a real nice guy, and he's always been very supportive of me. But, frankly, we never had much to discuss. If I talk about my studies or my clients from campus or my clinic, he listens politely, but I can tell that he doesn't get what I'm saying. I'm ashamed to admit that I'm not very interested in what he does at the machine shop where he works."

Jennifer has suggested to Jake that they try counseling to deal with their issues. She complained, "He wouldn't go. He said that he didn't have any issues. He said he didn't even know what I was talking about. Besides, he said, the counselor would probably just agree with me, anyway. He said that we were the same kind of people — college types."

Jennifer concluded by saying that she was contemplating getting a lawyer in order to file for divorce. She weepily acknowledged, "I feel terrible about this. I know that this will really hurt him. But I know that he hasn't been happy lately. He's starting to resent so many things, and I know he feels bad about resenting things. And I know that I'm not happy. Worse, I don't see how we can ever be closer. How did I get myself into a situation like this?"

Up to this point in our discussion of female mate selection, each chapter has quickly moved to theories or explanations for the conduct and, therefore, the choices of the women who have participated in my research. Following the classic rubric of nature versus nurture, we have stuck to the nurture side of the human condition. To a great extent, this is as it should be because, as a clinician, I am mostly interested in what my clients can actually do to regain control of their lives. I am personally a fan of the theories of Dr. William Glasser, generally known as *Reality Therapy*. It is also often referred to as *Choice Therapy*. That is the label I personally prefer and share with my clients. I believe that the word *choice* is a very liberating concept and one that most individuals do not readily or fully accept as a principle for their lives. This is understandable for many reasons. First, as I like to share with my clients, life is a little like a good news-bad news joke.

What's the good news? You can *choose* to do (or become) anything you want in this life. One of the great virtues of the United States is its freedoms. We truly have more opportunity and access to choice than anywhere else on earth.

What's the bad news? The bad news is that if you don't like something about your life, you have the ability and, therefore, the responsibility to change it. That burden, to some, is not so attractive. How many of us, for example, do not like to hear the soothing words, "It's not your fault?" Not many, I'm convinced. We all naturally like to be taken off the hook for our failings and misdeeds. And because it is naturally comforting to believe that we are not to blame for our life circumstances, I believe that we also automatically look outward to account for our undesirable conditions and situations.

Glasser's point is that *choice* is a two-sided coin of freedom and responsibility. This principle is, of course, not absolute. Certainly abused children, for example, lack the ability to choose to extricate themselves from their victimization. But women's shelters invest much of their focus on assisting battered women to make and choose the best options available to them in their distressful circumstances. These women are undeniably faced with difficult options, but their only salvation is in choosing the best possible avenue of remedy or escape. To suggest that there is no hope for such victims is to condemn them to the life they are leading.

But this chapter is addressing the last, and perhaps the most mysterious, of our six strands of female mate selection — *chemistry*. We will be looking at the nature side of the question of human behavior. It is the side that most clinicians of my training (professional counseling) know the least about. I believe that this is because we incorrectly assume that, if it is genetically influenced, there is little that we can do about it. It implies that Glasser's concept of choice does not apply if biological inclination is involved.

I often challenge this premise with my students and clients.

Imagine, for example, the following dialogue transpires between a client and her therapist (or between two friends, for that matter).

Dr. J	What did you do this weekend, Donna?
Donna	I went to a party.
Dr. J	How was it?
Donna	Not so hot.
Dr. J	What happened?
Donna	Nothing, really. I just sat in a corner while everyone else was laughing and having a good time.
Dr. J	Why did you do that?
Donna	Well, you know me, doctor. *I'm shy.*

Let's re-play the conversation. Read carefully.

Dr. J What did you do this weekend, Donna?

Donna I went to a party.

Dr. J How was it?

Donna Not so hot.

Dr. J What happened?

Donna Nothing really. I just sat in a corner while everyone else was laughing and having a good time.

Dr. J Why did you do that?

Donna Well, you know me doctor. *I have difficulty talking* to people.

Let's try it a third time. Once again, read carefully.

Dr. J What did you do this weekend, Donna?

Donna I went to a party.

Dr. J How was it?

Donna Not so hot.

Dr. J What happened?

Donna Nothing really. I just *chose* to sit in a corner while everyone else was laughing and having a good time.

Dr. J Why did you do that?

Donna I honestly don't know. I *often make bad choices* like that in social situations.

If you read through these three conversations quickly, you might think that the story was simply repeated over and over. There is a huge difference in the three narratives, however. The first Donna describes her unsatisfactory evening at the party as though the outcome was inevitable and irreconcilable. Why? Because she is "shy." Notice that that simple phrase is spoken as though the person using it has no control over the situation, even if it is painful or frustrating. We say "I'm shy" in much the same way that we might say "I'm tall" or "I have brown eyes." Nobody says "I choose to have brown eyes," or "I choose to be tall," because those physiological conditions do fall outside the realm of choice.

A careful listener (or a cognitive therapist) would describe the three conversations as being strikingly different, however. Donna #1 might be viewed as "stuck in a false belief," while Donna #2 might be considered a client as a work in progress. Donna #3 is definitely beginning to grasp the notion that behavior, to a significantly great extent, is within her control. Why? Well, the second Donna accounts her behavior as being based upon a *difficulty* she has. In this case, the difficulty is in talking to people. Notice that the word *difficulty* suggests that she does, at least potentially, have some degree of control or choice over her behavior at the party. *Difficult* is not the same as *impossible* or *inevitable*.

Donna #3's choice of words is significantly different. Observe how odd her third explanation sounds. "I just chose to sit in a corner..." Nobody talks like that! And yet, that is a very fair and accurate description of her behavior. Nobody has chained Donna to a couch away from the crowd. Nobody appears to have intimidated, threatened, or directed her to act as she did. Truly, Donna has *chosen* to distance herself from the festivities. Why? Because she believes that she is unable to join the party because of her shyness.

Donna #2 is acknowledging that her unhappy party experience was due to a behavior (speaking to others) that she struggles with. It implies a changeable or dynamic condition. Donna #1's lament (I'm shy) suggests a behavior that is outside her control, like her height or eye color. Hippocrates, Carl Gustav Jung, and the mother-daughter team of Meyers and Briggs from the University of Florida (authors of the Meyers-Briggs Type Indicator–MBTI) all agree that we come into the world with certain preprogrammed tendencies or inclinations. A temperament is defined as a genetically influenced personality trait. So, Donna's tendency to be quiet in social situations may have, in fact, some element of genetic predisposition. An inclination or genetic pre-disposition is not the same as a behavior that cannot be amended, however. The second Donna's description of her shyness as being a difficulty for her implies that she may be able to overcome that undesirable tendency with some thought, planning, and effort.

To further demonstrate that Donna's shyness can be overcome, let's go back to the original conversation with another whimsical, but pointed, twist to it.

> **Dr J**: Hi, Donna. I have some potentially good news for you. I just won the lottery: fifty-six million dollars. I decided that I would share part of my good fortune with my first client of the day and, guess what? That's you! You mentioned last week that you were going to attend a party tonight. I know that you have wanted to work on your tendency to be shy. With your permission, I'm going to ask your husband to record you at the party tonight. If you speak to all twelve of the people at the gathering tonight for at least ten minutes, I'll write you a check for one million dollars!

Talk about motivation! How many of us, given that opportunity, would earn the million? I believe that most of us would, irrespective of how shy we may see ourselves. It would take a very shy Donna to not earn the philanthropic bonus.

Sad to say, for both my clients and me, I haven't won the lottery. Donna's therapist cannot provide her with such an incentive. But an important principle has been established through this contrived example. Donna would almost certainly earn the million if it were available. But she would also almost certainly pass a polygraph test beforehand if questioned about being shy under normal, non-lottery winning circumstances. In other words, Donna (or most of us) truly believes that our frustrating or disappointing behaviors are the result of a trait over which we have no control. We believe that we cannot escape our undesirable traits because they appear to have been with us since birth. *This is simply not so.* Donna's earning of my imaginary one-million-dollar bonus proves that fact.

Donna #3's use of the words *choose* and *choice* suggests that she has come to understand that she is the master of her own conduct. Choosing different behaviors (for example, pushing herself toward more social, extroverted behavior) may be difficult, but definitely possible. Notice how, at the end of the Donna #3 example, she responds to her therapist's question with a truthful "I don't know." Is her shyness truly genetic, as Jung might suggest? Or is it learned tendency based upon her family of origin or some earlier childhood experience? This is certainly an area for Donna and her therapist to explore further. But an important principle has been established which will be liberating for Donna as she moves forward in her life. Donna #3 has progressed to a point of recognition that she is truly able to choose her behavior. She can now move forward to determine how she came to be shy in the first place or, perhaps even better, realize that finding why isn't important. As an adult, she now understands that her behavior is within her control.

Let's go back to our exploration of why women often choose ill-suited partners, and the topic of this chapter that is labeled as *chemistry*.

It is probably true that who we are initially drawn to may involve genetics or, in Freudian terms, some unconscious forces based upon our long-past childhood experiences. These tendencies or experiences may account for initial contacts, and the beginnings of relationships. To explore that idea, let's *eavesdrop* on the following afternoon discourse between two friends.

Imagine two women, Amy and Ellen, are having lunch together when an attractive stranger enters the eatery. The conversation begins:

> **Amy** Get a look at that guy. I'd sure like to meet him.
>
> **Ellen** Yes, he is a hunk. How come nobody who looks like that gets a job in our building?"

A few moments pass before another stranger enters the restaurant.

> **Ellen** Now there's a man I could get close to!
>
> **Amy** I agree. He's actually better looking than the first guy, but I still think that I'll stick with the first one.
>
> **Ellen** Listen to us! As if we have a choice as to which of the two guys we are going to date. Now tell me what happened to Gabby last night on *Housewives…*

In this imaginary friendly conversation, both women acknowledge that the two strangers walking into the restaurant are attractive. Neither woman knows either man. They have no knowledge of the men's background, educational level, or their marital status. The women don't know if they are wealthy or paupers. Are they interesting personalities or dullards? And yet both Amy and Ellen each express a clear preference toward one or the other of the two strangers. Perhaps even more significantly, Ellen expresses a preference for the second stranger while simultaneously acknowledging that the first man was actually the more handsome or attractive one.

Freudians or Jungians would probably speculate that the two men have triggered some unconscious, hidden experience which is drawing the women inexorably to their preferred stranger. Perhaps one man reminds Amy of her father or a favored uncle, although she does not realize it. Theorists such as Alfred Adler or Aaron Beck might imagine that the preference is occurring on a more conscious level. Perhaps the mode of dress or the presence or absence of facial hair influences Ellen's inclination toward the second man. In either case, the common principle at work from noted psychologists is that our choices are shaped by our experiences; early or late; conscious or unconscious.

The natural world of science may offer a very different view. Biologists and anthropologists suggest that perhaps our choices are actually hot-wired into us through the mysterious world of our DNA. Interestingly, even elements of the psychological world, the behaviorists, appear to be leaning in this direction as well. The behaviorist John Watson suggested that the notion of choice is really a misnomer — that we only believe that we are making a choice, a decision, about something. If we choose the red car over the black car, it is because in some primordial way we are predestined to do so. That same theoretician would pronounce that a woman is destined to be drawn to the fair-haired, muscular guy rather than the tall, aristocratic dark haired stranger.

While this train of thought probably wounds those of us who take pride in our cognitive abilities (and may offend our partners who believe that they had actually won us over), the biological world holds to its view that biochemistry has more to do with outcomes than rational thinking. Both biochemists and experimental psychologists have studied the influences of the male hormone, testosterone, on animal behavior for decades. We see female experimental rodents mounting other females when injected with increased levels of the male hormone. We observe positive correlations between testosterone levels of primates and their degree of both aggressive behavior and dominance within their peer group.

The *chemistry strand* should probably have been more accurately labeled the *biology strand*, but I have chosen to defer to the more colloquial language of our generation (i.e. "Those two snuggling in the corner appear to have a lot of chemistry between them.") In any case, the strand appears to account for relationship choices, such as Jennifer's in our introduction to this chapter, for which there does not appear to be a logical explanation. I list it as the last of the six strands, because it appears to account for relationship choices that cannot be attributed to other factors or the earlier strands. This strand also recognizes a significant (and currently popular) body of psychological thought: behaviorism.

None of us likes the notion that invisible, genetic forces are shaping our future relationships. We prefer the notion that we choose our mates and are able to decide on the person we will spend our life with. Once again, the good news is that we are able to make those decisions and determinations. Inclinations, whether they flow from our genes or our unconscious mind, are just that— inclinations. I believe that we are truly masters of our own destiny.

Let's summarize and review some of the major characteristics of this strand. That is, women who appear to be motivated by *chemistry*.

These women:

- make relationship choices that do not reflect similar backgrounds, interests, or educational levels

- do not appear to suffer from diminished self-concept or have a great need to please.

- may have strong beliefs about destiny, karma, or the immutability of genetic pre-disposition

- choose relationships that do not appear to lead to a specific type of partner. In other words, the male partner could be docile or outgoing; dominant or passive. The determination of attraction appears to flow from some unseen, unknown source and, upon reflection, these women describe markedly different partners if they have had more than one mismatched partner in the past.

- identify with this strand as they reflect on more than one past relationship, often reporting that the two (or more) *chemistry* choices were not similar to each other either. One was short and plain; the other taller and very handsome. One was highly educated; the other not.

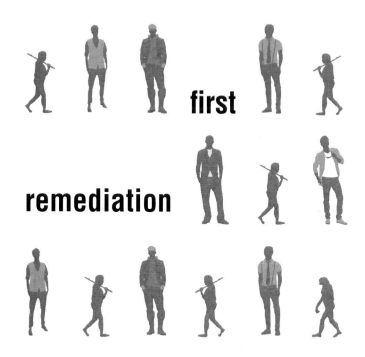

first

remediation

I know who I am, and I know that I am perfectly
capable of being whom I choose to be.

—Quixote

Recognize Your Personal Tendencies

Going back to the earliest periods of recorded history,
man has sought to account for behavioral tendencies —
personality traits, if you will. Before anything as structured
as learning theory or the concept of nurture (The concept
that our personality traits were shaped by our parents or
other sources of environmental influence.) was postulated,

the earliest observers of behavior looked to inborn characteristics or patterns to account for a person's actions.

Certainly, the medical science of biochemistry was millennia in the future, but early people observed that certain behaviors seemed to follow ancestral lines; that sons and daughters appeared to not only look like their parents, but tended to imitate their behavioral traits as well. Before the concept of genetic legacy (DNA) was formulated in the twentieth century, these tendencies were said to be passed on through the blood. Hence, the king would be referred to as being "of royal blood." Whether we allude to medieval royalty, to the concept of inherited divinity of an Egyptian pharaoh, or to the rigid, social-class structure of the caste system of even modern India, the belief is that personality traits (as well as other individual characteristics such as intelligence) are passed on through inheritance rather than learning or upbringing.

Often, we see this belief in determinism manifesting itself in everyday patterns of speech and common expressions. For example, how often have you heard someone say (or yourself say), "That's just the way I am?" We addressed this concept earlier in Chapter 6 when we used the example of the woman who lamented that she did not enjoy herself at a party, because she was shy. That simple phrase, *that's just the way I am,* serves as a defense, an excuse, and permission to do nothing to modify one's behavior or situation. Corollary statements might be, "I can't do that." rather than, "It would be difficult to do." or even, "I choose not to do that." resonate the same point.

It may be that I am guilty of pressing this point too strongly. As a therapist and professor, I often tell my counseling students that they are learning to become practitioners in *the change business.* I remind them that every client we see is looking for some change in their lives or is seeking ways to change the behavior of someone in his-her life (i.e., a spouse, a child, or even a boss). So my tendency to seek personal improvement comes to me honestly. But perhaps some of our personal tendencies and characteristics are ingrained. Or at least, they are admittedly very resistant to change. While we are all *a work in progress*, there is something to be said for the need to accommodate our tendencies even as we endeavor to modify them.

So, this seems to call for a compromise of sorts. Before we become what we aspire to be, it is essential that we come to understand who and what we are. This point is the basis for the title of this chapter. In coming to understand our tendencies, we are able to avoid the mistakes and behavioral inclinations that those attitudinal tendencies and personality traits may lead us to repeat.

Such as? Well, women who lack a positive sense of self need to recognize that they may be drawn to men who sadly reinforce their low opinion of themselves. Their low self-evaluations may lead them to fear rejection from more appropriate and worthy partners. Conversely, girls who have a tendency to wish to be helpful are invariably inclined toward men who demonstrate helplessness and who have become practiced in assuming a lamentable and pleading posture. Alluding to Chapter 3, female *excitement* seekers seem to be pulled toward the adrenalin-fueled, lovable underachievers. And, though we may be able to recognize the tendencies of others as outlined in this book, they may not be so easily recognizable in ourselves.

This recognizing of one's personal tendencies is not as easy as it may seem. Joseph Luft and Harry Ingram, the creators of the well known Johari Window, endeavored to give people a vehicle for self-understanding and insight with their instrument. The "window" divides personal awareness into four areas or panes. The panes reflect areas of self-understanding as well as areas of perception of us by others. The *window pane* includes information that we are aware of and others are aware of as well. For example, most people of my acquaintance are aware that I am a professor, have been happily married for many years, and have two adult children. Obviously, I am aware of those biographical facts as well. Another of the panes is labeled as *blind spots*. Blind spots involve personal traits which are unknown to us but visible to others. For example, a man whose toupee has, unbeknownst to him, become dislodged may pose a whimsical figure to others while he is bewildered by the snickering of those around him. The third pane, referred to as the *hidden self* includes information that the individual is aware of, but keeps hidden from others. Alcoholics, for example, may hide the true nature and extent of their drinking from others. The fourth window, described by Luft and Ingram as the *unknown pane*, holds information that neither the individual nor others are aware of, or can ascertain. A woman who has made a series of poor relationship choices may be genuinely bewildered by her flawed history of mate selection, and her circle of family and friends may not understand the basis for her dilemma either.

Using the Johari-window metaphor, therapists often suggest that human, personal progress involves expanding the public window while inversely shrinking the size of the other three. In other words, we should become more open and more honest with others and, of course, with ourselves.

Whether we are discussing blind spots or the unknown window panes, Luft and Ingram reflect that the goal of self-understanding and personal exploration is to shrink those windows and expand the size of the windows that include an understanding of ourselves. Greater self-understanding has a prophylactic quality; it insulates us from basically predictable mistakes once we come to grips with either our natural or learned inclinations.

Armed with such information, a woman who self assesses as being a *nurturer* can still feel compassion for a man who reaches out for her help but can also learn that, at least for her, helping historically has led her into an enabling situation. Additional, greater understanding takes her to a heightened understanding that while she may be willing to sacrifice her time, money and affection for the betterment of that male, she has come to realize that such excessive interventions actually keep the recipient of her ministrations from moving forward on his own energy and initiative. Like a parent who literally does her child's homework with the result that her son never learns long division, such women (with the absolute best of intentions) trap their adult "boys" in a cage of dependence and non-productivity.

To employ the Johari window metaphor once again, how do we achieve the mission of this chapter: to recognize our personal tendencies? As I have stated before in Chapter One, I often explain to my students that, contrary to what the public might assume, we counselors are not advisors. We are, instead, "professional mirror holders." Our job (and our skill) is in holding up a metaphorical mirror to our clients. By moving it to the left and to the right, as well as up and down, we use our talents to allow our clients to see themselves more clearly. Like a parent teaching a child how to ride a bike or an art teacher instructing a student how to shade in a shadow on a canvas, counselors ultimately expect their clients to *peddle* or *draw* on their own. We are endeavoring not to tell our clients *what* to think, but rather *how* to think. That is, how to approach a given problem or situation. In this case, the problem involves how to manage one's personal life. More specifically, this book addresses the process of choosing a partner successfully.

In order to proceed with this goal effectively, once again, self understanding comes into play. Learning to be one step ahead of ourselves is the key to accomplishing this feat. Let me suggest a form of practice here. This self improvement exercise is encapsulated in the old admonition, "Think before you speak."

A female client of mine, a successful saleswoman, once shared this instructive personal experience with me during a session. She had recently read what she considered to be an amusing story from a book about philosophy and humor. A chapter in the book addressed the concept of eternity and contained what she viewed as an amusing quip: Having enjoyed the story, she decided to pass it on to a group of her friends over lunch.

It narrated: A man is informed by his physician that he is terminally ill and has only six months to live. He asks his doctor if there is anything he can do. She responds, "Yes, you can marry a tax accountant."

The man asked, "How will that help with my medical condition?"

The doctor replies, "It won't help with your illness, but it will make six months seem like an eternity."

Most of the women at the lunch table chuckled, but one woman was, in fact, a tax accountant. She was clearly offended by the joke, remarking, "You could tell that story and substitute tax accountant with attorney, or librarian, or even saleswoman."

"Oops!" my client explained. She understood that she had messed up. While it was not her intention to amuse the other women at the table at someone else's expense, she had nevertheless done so.

Was my client's tax accountant friend overly sensitive? I don't think so. It was my client's obligation to be aware of her audience and modify the story to avoid giving offense, or perhaps skip the narration of the anecdote entirely. Advising the accountant to "not be so touchy" would have been insulting and inappropriate. Blaming the victim is always out of line.

So, the aforementioned self-improvement exercise involves thinking before speaking or, when it comes to relationships, thinking before acting. For example, women who recognize that the *desire to be* nurtured-strand describes them must come to see that praise and attentiveness may, in fact, be possessiveness and controlling behavior. Or women who see the *control* strand as applicable to them need to perceive in themselves an inclination to pick weaker partners that they have an ability to dominate or manipulate.

The dictum to recognize one's personal tendencies is truly easier said than done. Looking into the metaphorical mirror isn't always a pleasurable exercise. It is, however, always worthwhile and instructive for those with the courage to do so.

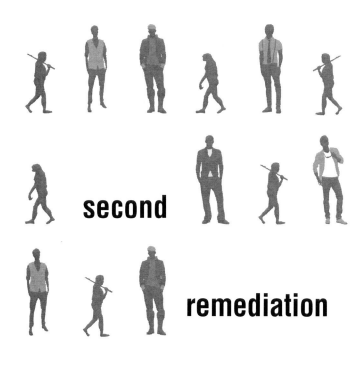

second

remediation

Don't dream it; be it.
—Rocky Horror Picture Show

Recognize That Your Sense of Self Determines Your Direction and Choices

In earlier chapters we discussed the first strand, low self-esteem, and reviewed the historical context of the self-esteem movement. We reviewed the misinterpretation of Dr. Spock's messages regarding parenting, as well as the counterpoint of Dr. Martin Seligman's message that self-esteem cannot be given but, rather, is a product of the individual's achievements. We also discussed the role, via Carol Gilligan's theories, that the dominant value system of women as helpers affects their decisions regarding their partners.

For better or worse, self-esteem persists as an important concept in modern behavioral thought and is a key term in our understanding of who we are and why we do the things we do. In earlier chapters, I explained the metaphor of the counselor as professional mirror-holder. As is true of many professionals, the ultimate goal of the practitioners is to put themselves out of business. Nutritionists, for example, should hope that the client will eventually assume appropriate eating habits and will no longer require their dietary input and suggestions. Personal fitness instructors may expect that their customer learns how to develop and implement a fitness regimen without their daily encouragements and direction. Similarly, the professional clinician should follow a treatment plan that leads to the client ultimately holding his-her own mirror.

Mirror-holding is a demanding endeavor. It is definitely not for the faint hearted. However cosmetically gifted any of us may be, taking a long, serious look into the metaphorical mirror can be daunting. To demonstrate this point, let's engage in an exercise that is literal (tangible) rather than metaphorical…if you dare.

The exercise is as simple as it may prove unnerving. Tomorrow morning, when you rise and begin to prepare for your day with your daily ablutions, take *one extra minute* and simply gaze into the mirror above your sink. Look into your own eyes. You are not examining your face. You aren't noticing dermatological flaws in your complexion. You are, quite simply, looking at you. No averting of your glance. You will be somewhat stunned by the experience; I assure you.

At this point, many of our readers will be inclined to think: "That's dumb. I do that every morning. What's the point?" I beg to differ. Every morning we all stare into the mirror to check out how our makeup is going on. Or to see if we have given ourselves a clean shave. Or that we have brushed our hair into the desired coif. Or if our wrinkles (some of us prefer *"character lines")* have extended themselves. These cosmetic evaluations are not what this experiment is all about.

The suggested sixty-second exercise is for you to look at yourself in an analytical, non-physical way. What do you see? Do you see someone you like? Someone you are proud to be? Or are your reactions less positive?

Whatever we see through that exercise, the result of that self-examination is highly significant. As a clinician, it is my belief that everything we do flows from our self-perception: our sense of self. When I present my findings to live audiences, I often refer to my clinical *snowman*. It is represented below.

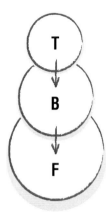

I've drawn this hundreds of times for clients and students. While the drawing may
be an original representation of the principles it outlines, the concepts it represents
are hardly unique or originating from your
author. It is my concrete way of explaining
to clients, students, and audiences the basic
method and point of view of cognitively-
oriented therapy. As the illustration suggests
"T leads to be B and B leads to F." T stands
for our thoughts or beliefs. B represents our
behaviors or actions. F describes our feelings
or emotional reactions to what we do.

Clients never come to see a therapist because of what they
are thinking. Nobody initially expresses their frustrations
over their self-defeating beliefs. Clients seek therapists,
voluntarily or under duress, as a result of their actions
or perhaps their resulting emotions. Clients enter into
treatment because their behavior has gotten them into
trouble with their spouse, or their employer or, perhaps,
the law. They seek help because of the threat of impending divorce, or job loss, or a possible conviction for some
criminal offense. Or they seek relief from feelings of
depression or anxiety. Or perhaps their ill-temper has led
them into untenable situations. In other words, people
seek help because of what they have done (behaviors) or
because of their negative emotions (feelings).

I explain to my new clients that, while we will hopefully address the behaviors that led them to seek help, we
must first determine, then address, the thoughts or beliefs
that fathered those actions. I explain to clients that we
will seek to ameliorate their negative feelings through a
process of examining the thoughts that led to their behav-

iors. Cognitively-oriented therapy seeks to identify the thoughts or beliefs that, in turn, ultimately generate their negative emotions.

Imagine that a woman, Jessica, receives her third drunk-driving ticket. She is ashamed of this and is justifiably worried about the legal consequences. She is ordered into counseling by the sentencing judge. The clinician asked Jessica about her treatment goals. She responds:

Jessica	I know I have to get a handle on my drinking.
Counselor	What does that mean exactly?
Jessica	I guess it means that I can't afford to drink and drive; that I have to cut down on my drinking.
Counselor	If I had interviewed you after your first or second arrest and asked you the same question, how would you have responded?
Jessica	Gee, I'm not sure. I think I would have said that I needed to be more careful with my drinking.
Counselor	If you had been hooked up to a lie detector back then, would you have passed?
Jessica	Definitely. Only an idiot wouldn't care if she got another one of these.
Counselor	So what happened?
Jessica	I don't know. I just screwed up again. And again.

Notice that Jessica focused on her behavior rather than her thoughts or beliefs. Since no one gets arrested every time he-she drinks and drives, Jessica probably (but erroneously) believed that her drinking was under control, and that each *successful* (non-arrest) incident of drinking and driving proved that her drinking was under control when it obviously wasn't.

As I whimsically point out to clients, "Five out of six players of Russian roulette report a favorable outcome." No sane person would construe that statistical fact to indicate that Russian roulette was a safe, yet very exciting pastime. Getting a *click* rather than a *boom* simply indicates temporary good fortune, not safety. Similarly, drinking and driving, even when not apprehended, represents dangerous conduct. Denial allows the problematic drinker to overlook, to deny, that clear reality.

While Jessica is sincere in her desire to avoid another arrest and conviction, her cognitive game plan is ill-conceived. Notice that her initial plan was "to cut down" (manage) on her drinking. Most addiction counselors would agree that some members of society, either due to genetic or environmental-learned factors, would be better served through abstinence rather than attempting to control or limit their consumption. While Jessica criticizes her own behavior, a cognitive therapist would invite her to take a closer look at her beliefs about her own drinking. The therapist would point out that her behavior flowed from her current thoughts or beliefs. Specifically, Jessica's thoughts ("I need to cut down on my drinking") led to her behavior

(Jessica still drank). Continuing to drink eventually led to her second and third arrest.

Jessica's focus has been on her behavior when it needs to be on her beliefs. If Jessica's new thoughts were, "I don't know why, but drinking seems to get me in trouble. Maybe I need to quit." that new thought would have led her to abstinence. If Jessica adopted that belief, what would definitely be the outcome? Obviously, if she never drank, it would be impossible for her to get a drunk-driving ticket. And, back to my illustrative snowman, what would the emotional consequences of that new thought and behavior pattern be? There would be no more embarrassment, frustration, and pain associated with another alcohol-related conviction. While no one could guarantee that Jessica would be arrested again if she chose to continue to drink, it could be guaranteed that she could never be arrested for drinking and driving again if she terminated her use.

The point of this example is clear. While most of us tend to dwell on our actions or emotions, the origin of both lies in our thoughts/beliefs about ourselves. Let's go back to women and their choice of partners and the mirror exercise.

What thoughts do we harbor about ourselves, and how do they either serve us or defeat us? Consider that all of our beliefs and thoughts about ourselves fit into one of two categories. Our thoughts about ourselves are either accurate or inaccurate. Inaccurate thoughts, perhaps based upon false or critical messages we received about ourselves, or maybe from critical or abusive past partners, need to be rejected. How? Back to the mirror.

> Imagine that you are making two lists below. One list catalogs accurate perceptions of self. Note that this list will include both positive and negative qualities. The other list includes beliefs and self-perceptions that are not factual or supported by the opinions of most others; not just a critical few. The task,

therefore, is to eliminate or erase all inaccurate beliefs and perceptions while accepting (or working for improvement) on those beliefs found to be accurate.

Accurate Beliefs	Inaccurate Beliefs
1	1
2	2
3	3

When you look into your literal and metaphorical mirror, what do you see? You may have been told you were stupid or lazy by an abusive partner, but are you? Look closely and be honest with your appraisal. If your job performance and work ethic around your home would suggest the opposite, then it is important to make the conscious decision to reject the labels of *stupid* or *lazy*. Also, note your own tendency to accept negative characterizations of you, even when you are cognitively aware that they aren't true. (i.e. "I get consistently positive evaluations at work." or "My friends always compliment me on how beautiful my home is.") In other words, the objective data about ourselves clearly contradicts the feelings we have or the negative input we may be receiving from an abusive partner. As you gaze into your mirror, does it make more sense to accept the data from many more objective sources or from the one person who seems determined (for whatever unknown reason) to bring you down?

On the other hand, at times, the metaphorical mirror confirms the painful truth that some of our negative self-perceptions are accurate. Where do we go with those painful insights? How do we address the situation when the objective data confirms some negative thoughts about ourselves?

As I mentioned in the Naiah chapter, some people *do guilt* in the same way that some addicts do drugs. The solution? *Stop doing that!* In other words, stop *doing* guilt. Instead, do something else. Do something positive. Instead of feeling guilty about eating junk food or smoking, engage in healthier behavioral patterns. Drive past the fast food outlets, and allow yourself to feel good about doing so. Or buy the patch to help you with nicotine withdrawal.

At this point, allow me to engage in a slight digression. Let's talk about guilt. Guilt is a little like the proverbial good-news-bad-news joke. What's the good news about guilt? Well, guilt flows from our conscience. People who lack a conscience are commonly referred to as psychopaths or sociopaths. These are very scary individuals because they don't feel bad when they hurt others. While they may fool us somewhat because they may demonstrate strong emotion as they are about to be incarcerated or executed for their crimes, there is still a difference between their emotions and the feelings of others. The psychopath's feelings (probably real rather than faked) are strictly for themselves. In other words, they don't feel bad because of what they did or who they hurt. They simply are upset because they were caught and are about to be punished. They are not exhibiting emotion flowing from guilt. Thankfully, the pain that most of us feel is linked to our sense of responsibility for wrongdoing. So, guilt feelings reflect a conscience, and that's good.

If guilt reflects a conscience, then what's bad about it? The real downside to guilt is its paralyzing effect. It immobilizes us, not energizes us. There is a fairness, a justice to guilt as well. A guilt-driven individual may ruminate, "I made a mistake, but I feel terrible about it." That seems fair. And it is. But notice that the focus is on *feeling bad*, and not on *changing behavior*. It is obviously far better to amend one's negative actions rather than simply feeling guilty about them.

To reverse this trend of guilt and resulting paralysis, a change of thought is essential. When an individual recognizes guilty feelings, those feelings must serve as an incentive or motivation for change. The new thought pattern might look more like this: I did something that I shouldn't have. I feel guilty about it, and I guess that's good, because it shows that I have a conscience. Recognizing that, in the past, I've done little about that other than becoming self-critical, it's time to reverse that old pattern. What can I do to make up for my mistake? How can I amend the situation or, more specifically, my behavior? (Reminder: Notice how this reflects the progression with the snowman. A new thought or belief leads to a new behavior or action). In this new train of thought, our guilty feelings are used as a catalyst for action, not paralysis.

Enough on guilt. Let's go back to the issues raised through our self-analytical gazes into the mirror. To summarize, we have suggested that we make the cognitive decision to reject images that we know are not accurate. Conversely, we have decided to change past behaviors or patterns that we have determined to be negative but accurate when we look into our metaphorical mirror. What I've just recommended is a change in behavior. The message of this chapter appeared to involve beliefs. Isn't the above focus on behavior, contrary to this chapter's premise?

Not really. When the mirror exercise reveals some painful truths about ourselves, it also hides the latent thought patterns that sustain those negative behavioral facts. For example, every adult smoker is trapped in a belief system that keeps the smoker in a behavioral pattern that almost all of them would love to escape. Only the most fact-rejecting of smokers cling to the belief that, magically, the harmful, carcinogenic effects of smoking will pass over them like the biblical angel of death will skip over their house forever. So why, then, do smokers continue an expensive, offensive, and medically near-suicidal behavior when most will candidly acknowledge a desire to terminate this self-destructive (and smelly!) behavior?

To obtain the answer, listen carefully to the commonly expressed views of smokers themselves. For example, a smoker might lament: "I can't quit." or, "I'm under a lot of stress now. I'll quit later." or, "I have no will power. I'm weak." These statements, while almost certainly truthfully expressed, are nevertheless inaccurate. Each statement suggests a more or less permanent, immutable condition. They are expressed in absolute terms. "I can't quit." is an absolute statement. Conversely, the statement, "It's difficult to quit." at least opens the door to the possibility of change. Alternatively, "So far, I've chosen to continue to smoke." suggests total ownership, if not control, over the undesirable, smoking habit. Sadly, no one speaks in the manner of our third example! But we all should.

So the smoker is not trapped in an undesirable habit (behavior) so much as she is embroiled in a pattern of self-defeating, negative thought. Smokers need to change the belief that they are incapable of change or that the only stress management resource is nicotine or that they suffer from an irreconcilable character flaw (weakness).

What then, is the flawed belief of the capable woman who continues to make poor relationship choices or to remain in an unsatisfying or abusive current relationship? The answer to that is found in the belief system of each of those women. But the point of this chapter is that the source of these unsatisfying relationship situations lies in the belief system of the woman who possesses them.

Simply stated, if we can only change our thinking, we will, in fact, change our lives.

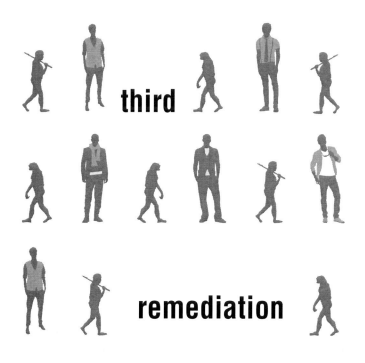

third

remediation

The mind acts like an enemy for those who do not control it.

—Gita

Recognize That Personal Beliefs and Ideas are the Basis of all Behavioral Choice

Certainly, the operative of this chapter flows naturally from the concepts laid out in the previous chapter on self-concept. Self-concept is basically a set of specific ideas we have about ourselves. Some might assume that chapters 8 and 9 may be somewhat redundant (i.e. Isn't one's sense of self (chapter 8) basically a reflection of her-his thoughts and beliefs (chapter 9)? They are certainly closely related but not synonymous. While our sense of self does reflect our thoughts and beliefs about ourselves, we have many more thoughts and beliefs that do not involve us directly. Like what, for example?

Well, we have very different ideas or notions about other people. We have fairly specific (or vague) views about God, religion, and spirituality. We have a generalized view of life and philosophical orientation. Would we describe ourselves as essentially optimistic or pessimistic? Are we basically trusting or cautious? Thrifty or economically impulsive? And so on. All of these issues aren't directly related to our sense of ourselves but, of course, bear on our life decisions and outcomes.

Thomas A. Harris, the author of the immensely popular book of the 70's on transactional analysis, *I'm OK; You're OK*, posits that we all approach life from one of four basic attitudinal formations (Harris labels them as "life positions.") reflecting our beliefs about ourselves and others. Harris coins the term "OK" to describe our overall feelings either about ourselves or about others. "OK-ness," as reflected in both the book's title and Harris' text, implies an essentially balanced and positive view of an individual or her world. "Not OK-ness" conversely demonstrates a skeptical or critical or even depressive view of self or others.

In Harris' metaphorical view of the world and life, there are three unhealthy or dysfunctional life positions while there exists only one balanced and productive view of life. The three flawed views are:

> I'm OK; you're not OK
> I'm not OK; you're OK
> I'm not OK; you're not OK

The "I'm OK; you're not OK" life position reflects a critical or suspicious view of the world. Other people are not to be trusted. Caution is generally called for in almost all situations. When others fail us or disappoint us, we are not surprised. Their shortcomings simply confirm our view of the world in general. Their dominant emotion is skepticism and suspicion. Individuals from this life position see themselves as essentially functional (OK) but are stranded in a world populated by either incompetent or wily characters. Caution and vigilance are required on the part of the individual to avoid the negative impact that others may visit upon them. Their dominant emotion is either suspicion or exasperation.

The polar opposite of the above is the "I'm not OK; you're OK" life position. To these sad individuals, life and the world is a fun event; a party to which they have not been invited. With noses pressed against the window of the banquet hall of life, they envy those attractive, intelligent, and popular people who frolic within while they suffer in the cold outside due to their unworthiness. Their dominant emotion is sadness and rejection.

The third unacceptable position is "I'm not OK; you're not OK." These individuals share the critical nature of the above first position, but also see themselves as part of the negative world. They appear to be stuck in a grim, existential philosophy that opines, "Life is a garbage sandwich, and every day we all take a bite." They are suspicious of others but don't feel very good about themselves either. A sense of futility and resignation may best characterize them.

Fortunately, there is a healthy and functional option, according to Thomas Harris. The "I'm OK; you're OK" life position is not a Pollyanna philosophy. It recognizes that caution is, at times, needed with others. It also takes a realistic of view of self. But the essential orientation involves optimism and a positive view of self and others. This life position enables its adherents to move forward in their life pursuits without the debilitating attitudes expressed in the first three life positions. The dominant emotion of those from this "life position" is optimism and a forward-thinking posture.

What's the connection between this chapter's message about personal thoughts and beliefs and Harris' TA life position theory? Clearly, the beliefs expressed in the first three unacceptable life positions could be characterized as roadblocks to moving forward with life's goals. As it relates to relationship choice, we can see a positive correlation between some of the TA life positions and the strands discussed in the first six chapters of this book.

For example, Terri, from our first chapter which explored self-esteem issues, could be said to be coming from an "I'm not OK; you're OK" life position. While she was described as an attractive woman and successful professional, that clearly was not her sense of herself. Most of us would probably describe her husband, Bob, as a loafer who was unworthy of Terri, but she did not see herself or that relationship that way.

Conversely, Kathleen, from the chapter on control, clearly is seeing her life and those around her from a diametrically opposite position than Terri. Kathleen could be said to be coming from an "I'm OK; you're not OK" position, at least as it relates to her underachieving husband. It could be argued that Kathleen has derived some satisfaction from having a dependent husband. It establishes her role as the leader and decision-maker in her family and reaffirms her personal "I'm OK" view of herself. If her husband were more functional, his stability and achievement might challenge her "Not OK" perception of him. One might also theorize that a person like Kathleen is likely to have a jaundiced view of her boss at work and perhaps her children as well.

In earlier chapters, we spoke of the belly button metaphor and the concept of locus *of control*. While being an *innie* or an *outie* was not quite the same as having an internal or external locus of control, both sets of concepts dealt with an individual's overview of life and the world. In that sense, each of the strands described in this book's first six chapters at least implies a dispositional attitude about the women whose poor relationship choices were motivated by the topic of that chapter.

Therefore, as women seek to learn from their past poor-partner choices (or prevent making such choices in the future), they would be well-served to look inward to ascertain their overviews of the world, others, and themselves. Women with an "I'm OK; you're OK" view of self and others are more likely to seek partners who are both healthy individuals and a good match for them. Those who fail to recognize their own diminished sense of self and/or others are likely to be susceptible to choose poorly and, ultimately, deny themselves the relationship, joy, and satisfaction that they seek.

As a man thinketh in his heart, so is he.

Proverbs 23:7

fourth

remediation

Assumptions are the termites of relationships.

—H. Winkler

Learn and Recognize the Differences Between Healthy Versus Unhealthy Relationships

Curiously, relationships may be an area of human endeavor in which others have a better perception of a relationship situation than those in the pairing may have. How many times have we sat on the observational sideline, recognizing that a good friend or sibling is blissfully heading down the train tracks of life into a tunnel with a single headlight hurtling toward her? Picking herself up after the inevitable collision, we are astounded to hear her lament, "I never saw that coming."

Our hypothetical friend or relative is not lacking in intelligence or wisdom normally. If the roles were reversed, she would be able to predict such wreckage for one of her acquaintances or relatives. So why is it that we are so blind to our own mistakes, yet reasonably prescient about others' missteps? The answer may have to do with some of the topics we have already discussed, such as low self-esteem or an excessive need to be a caretaker, but it may also flow from our distorted view of love and caring, at least when we are emotionally involved.

Literature, songs, and movies are flooded with simplistic, fatalistic, or inane examples and models of what love relationships should look like. Stanley and Stella Kowalski, in Tennessee Williams' *A Streetcar Named Desire,* play out an intense relationship that demonstrates more passion and dependence than real liking or intimacy. George Clooney's character from *Up in the Air* reflects a view that detachment allows all to lighten our life's backpack. Shakespearean sonnets and the poetry of Robert Burns take on an idyllic tone of devotion without a hint of sexuality attached to them. Danielle Steele novels basically equate sexual attraction and lust with love.

At one point in the history of cinema, *Titanic* was the all-time, box-office champ. Aside from the movie being about a big boat sinking, *Titanic* was essentially the story of Jack and Rose (Leonardo DeCaprio and Kate Winslet). As many will recall, the story is told in flashback through Rose's one hundred-year-old eyes. She is accompanied on a deep sea diver's search for her lost gem, given to her by her emotionally distant and cruel fiancé. Through other scenes and photographs shown in the film, Rose obviously survived the tragedy, married, and had children and grandchildren as she is shown to be in the company of her granddaughter on the expeditionary ship looking for the diamond. Essentially, we learn that Rose had lived a full life, presumably with a long-term husband, and served as a matriarch to unknown numbers of children and grandchildren.

But what was the emotional message of *Titanic*, and what relevance does that have in our discussion of love relationships? Let's examine the story of Jack and Rose a little more closely. First of all, Rose never met Jack until some time after the giant ship's sailing. That means that the two young people knew each other for less than four days (Note: Titanic sailed on April 10, 1912, and sank on April 14 of the same year). And yet, the emotional message of this immensely popular movie was that the defining love relationship of Rose's life was her three or four day encounter with Jack Dawson, a young man with whom she had nothing in common. Were Rose a real rather than fictional character, one would wonder how Rose's husband of who knows how many years would have felt about that revelation about his wife's prior relationship? And yet, as movie goers, we eat up that sexy morsel of emotional drivel.

One could argue, "It's just a movie; just entertainment." True enough, but something is shaping our attitudes about love, and the results are not positive. The divorce rate in America is roughly fifty percent. And that figure does not include the number of failed serious relationships (co-habitation/live-in situations) that do not sustain themselves.

My unsupported guesstimate would be that our success rate in sustaining relationships wallows somewhere in the twenty-five percent range. And of those, how many could truly be characterized as healthy, intimate pairings?

If I have painted a dim and grim picture, I propose to offer some hope as well. It is, in fact, the mission of this chapter. The solution, I believe, is in education. And education can occur at any stage in life and through various venues. Teaching children and adolescents the basics of love is not inappropriate. Universities should be addressing this topic as well, irrespective of the discipline being trained, as love relationships affect all workers, regardless of their profession. Adult learners can gain insight into their personal life through works such as this one or myriad others. Yet we, at times, cling to the belief that matters of the heart cannot be quantified or examined in any rational way. I beg to differ.

Virtually any profession invokes basic relationship psychology as a facet of its training. Any company, for example, that involves a marketing function spends huge amounts in training its sales force in effective communication and skillful listening techniques to identify the attitudes and preferences of its client base, and in "reading" the customer to maximize sales results. As a counselor/educator in the business of training future clinicians, my students are grounded in body language, active listening skills, and in discerning the belief systems and attitudes of their clients. Even auto engineers and designers are attentive to ergonomics and the aesthetic appeal for customers concerning both the exterior and interior of their vehicles.

And yet, in personal relationships, many under the age of forty would rather text than talk. This is the case even when there is no apparent barrier to spoken conversation. In *Up in the Air*, we see Clooney's character engaging in sexy text repartee with his girlfriend rather than have a phone conversation as they engage in pillow talk from their respective beds, separated by hundreds of miles. When he discovers that his lover has a husband and children, he is shocked. Should he be? Not really, since he never really got to know her through the conventional means of communication: talking.

Robert Sternberg, the noted psychologist, postulates the concept of consummate love. He explains that a total (consummate) love relationship is demonstrated by a balanced triangle with the three sides representing the qualities of *passion, intimacy, and commitment*. Different love relationships can involve only one of these three qualities. For example, a relationship that is all passion is labeled *infatuation*. A relationship that is only intimate could be referred to as *friendship* or *companionate love*. Sometimes a relationship may involve a combination of two of the three elements of Sternberg's triangle. For example, a relationship that possesses both passion and intimacy but lacks commitment is coined *romantic* love. If two people meet on a singles cruise and decide to have the ship's captain marry them after six days at sea, *passion and a commitment* are motivating this union, but clearly they do not know each other. There is no true intimacy in this situation. Sternberg calls such a union *fatuous* (foolish) love.

If we refer back to Jack and Rose in *Titanic*, we see the stereotypical, romantic relationship. There could be no commitment between them as they were together for only three or four days. If there were no iceberg, would they have moved into a committed relationship? Who can honestly say?

Ironically, most Americans would see a total relationship as synonymous with romantic love. In other words, we often see the commitment side of Sternberg's triangle as not particularly attractive. As youth-obsessed as we tend to be in our culture, we don't see an elderly couple still together after many decades as very inspirational or desirable. Dying in the icy waters of the North Atlantic, Jack never got old. He never left his underwear lying on the bedroom floor. He never generated the inevitable byproduct of Rose's bean salad. And so on. Essentially, Sternberg's theory would suggest that our culture does not understand love in the sense that he renders it as a balance of three very different functions and dynamics: *passion, intimacy, and commitment.*

Just as this author believes that Sternberg's triangle should be taught to our youth, I believe that every girl and woman who has experienced an imbalanced and unsatisfying relationship would benefit by taking a fearless inventory of her past and present choices. As suggested earlier during the discussion of my snowman, our relationship decisions and choices are dictated by the beliefs we hold and the knowledge we possess (or lack) about love.

If, for example, we hold to the view that a true love relationship would have us on the edge of our love seat forever, then we are doomed to go from one interlude to the next, because we are confusing passion (infatuation) with love. The couple who decided to wed after their whirlwind romance at sea is likely to learn later that they have little in common.

This book and this chapter do not claim to teach its readers all there is to know about love. A pre-school teacher who shares the alphabet with a kindergartner cannot claim to have turned their charge into a novelist.

But that educator can rightly claim to have moved that child in the right direction. That teacher can take credit for pointing her students toward the benefits of writing and reading. I encourage those who reflect on this chapter to consider examining more on the subject of love and to dispassionately (yes, without overt emotion!) analyze their views and beliefs about the topic itself. Think of it as risk (and tragedy/disaster) management.

A life unexamined is not worth living.

—Thoreau

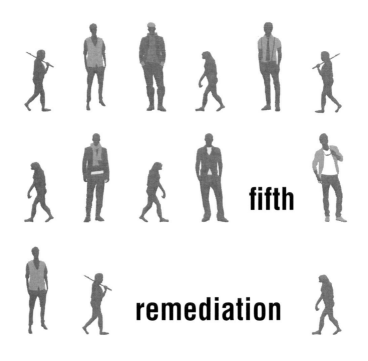

fifth

remediation

It's not hard to make good decisions when
you know what your values are.

—Roy Disney

While Biology Is a Powerful Influence, Individuals Retain the Ability to Shape Their Behavioral Choices

Before beginning a more detailed discussion of the major premise of this chapter, let's define some terms. While the heading for this chapter makes reference to *biology*, the more common colloquial term for immediate attraction to another person is *chemistry*. I'm referring to the highly emotional, visceral draw that we, at times, have for another, although we know little, if anything, about that individual at that time. It is Hollywood's love at first sight. It is Rhett Butler's desire for Scarlett, even though he clearly recognizes her vanity and manipulative nature. And it is Scarlett's persistent yen for Melanie's husband, Ashley, while the obviously more attractive Rhett (Clark Gable) is waiting to give her both love and the status she values.

Certainly the movie industry could be held to account for the perpetuation of such romantic mindless love but is the silver screen creating such an emotion-driven value system or merely accepting its existence and building stories around the phenomena? No matter. Anyone who ever experienced a high school crush can attest that something very real and powerful hits us, seemingly on a very physical level.

The physical love-fuel that energizes us is pheromones. Pheromones are defined by Wikopedia as "chemicals acting outside the body of the secreting individual to impact the behavior of the receiving individual." While the research into this phenomenon as it relates to human-mate selection is less than definitive, perhaps producing "more heat than light," it is nevertheless worth considering. More concrete evidence exists that speaks to the effect of odors on insects and even mammals, such as horses. For example, it is well known among breeders of thoroughbreds that mares are easily identifiable as being "in season" (ovulating) by their docile, receptive behavior. Conversely, those same female equines typically exhibit annoyance and resistance when approached by interested stallions when they are not primed for reproductivity. (Is this the horsey equivalent of, "Not tonight. I have a headache?)

The evidence that humans react to stimuli that is not consciously identifiable is not conclusive. Nevertheless, the research that is the basis of this book (Over three hundred surveys completed by women who have experienced a disappointing relationship with males who did not appear to be their functional equal.) revealed many female respondents who genuinely were puzzled by their choices. These women could not identify themselves as *nurturers* or *low self-esteem* persons or *controllers,* or with the other variables listed in earlier chapters. They just said, "There was something about him that drew me to him."

The essential difference that distinguishes humans from the rest of the living world is our brain. That complex and powerful engine of thought enables us to behave with more than instinct, even while we may share some of those instinctual, perhaps biochemical, tendencies with lower life forms. Simply stated, we have the ability to *think and decide*, while other creatures simply react to the innate forces within them.

To demonstrate the distinction between built-in behavioral tendencies and the human ability to choose certain actions, imagine that you recently received notice that you have been summoned for jury duty. For many, this is a troubling intrusion upon our normal routine as a homemaker or career person. For others, like me who is a frustrated non-lawyer, it provides the alluring opportunity to enter into the work space of Perry Mason, Robert Kardashian (Kim's father was one of O.J.'s attorneys), Allan Dershowitz, or the various fictional attorneys from John Grisham novels. In any case, jury duty places most of us into unfamiliar territory.

Suppose that the case you are called to serve on involves rape. Your trial does not involve the potentially confusing details surrounding a date rape situation. This trial involves strangers. A woman is attacked walking to her car in a parking lot as a shopping mall is closing for the evening. She has been brutally violated. The assaulter was identified via his license plate and apprehended shortly thereafter. DNA evidence taken from the victim via the rape kit clearly identifies the suspect as the assaulter. During the trial at which you are one of the twelve jurors, the defense attorney makes no attempt to deny his client's involvement in the attack. Instead, his defense is based upon biological, physical evidence. The assaulter's lawyer argues that his client suffers from an inordinately, high-level of testosterone; that his aberrant conduct is the result of irresistible sexual impulses and desires. Several expert witnesses, (forensic pathologists, geneticists, and internists) describe at length the normal levels of testosterone for average males, in contrast to the higher levels of the defendant. The defense attorney argues that his client is truly a victim of his own atypical, biochemical makeup.

You and your eleven peers now retire to the deliberation room. What is your leaning? Acquittal or conviction? Guilty or innocent? I believe that, for most reasonable and free-thinking individuals, such a defense argument will not dissuade the jury from holding the perpetrator accountable for his sexual violence and hostility.

Imagine that, once again as a juror, you drew into a different case. This trial involves a different form of violence. This case involves a brawl in a restaurant parking lot over a parking space. Two drivers approach the same empty space at about the same time in the crowded lot.

Horn honking escalates into driver side windows being rolled down to allow for angry heads to protrude, spewing threats and vitriol. One of the two drivers takes the dispute to the next level. He exits his car, approaches his adversary, and punches the other driver three times through the open window. Police are summoned. Charges are filed, and two months later, you are in the jury box listening to arguments.

This time, the defense attorney for the parking lot assailant argues that his client is the victim of an inherited aggressive personality. He cites a family history of hostile behavior, with grandparents and his client's father having been convicted over the years of various violent crimes and incidents. Psychologists report the results of psychological tests and personality inventories that describe the defendant's propensity for aggression. As a juror, you are asked to acquit the defendant based upon his bad genes. Once again, what is your inclination in the jury room? Do you agree with the defense attorney that his client should be released because he has a bad temper? It is probable that most of us would not excuse that defendant based upon that argument.

What do these two exercises in hypothetical jurisprudence have to do with female-mate selection? Simply this: in both of the above cases, the juror is asked to excuse sexual or other physical violence based upon some inherited, genetic predisposition. It claims that we are all victims of tendencies that we have no control over. As we have surmised, these arguments would probably not convince most jurors.

Why not? Because most of us expect, as members of a civilized society, that our fellow citizens control their behavior. We may concede that one man has a greater sex drive than another man, but we do not excuse sexual violence based upon even documented evidence that prove hormonal variations exist. Put simply, we expect people to control themselves. Similarly, as in the second hypothetical court case, we recognize that some of us are more quick-tempered than others. Some of us tend to be phlegmatic while others are more mercurial. Nevertheless, we are unlikely to excuse parking lot assaults based upon short-tempered tendencies.

Still, there does appear to be a renaissance of an older belief that mate selection may be influenced by unconscious, undetectable, sensory stimuli. Specifically, scents. The premise is that, like other members of the animal kingdom, *Homo sapiens* make mating choices based upon olfactory messages we receive from potential partners. The phenomenon is clear among mammals when we observe the flaring of nostrils among cattle and horses during mating. Cosmetic firms market musk scents as aphrodisiacs. Apparently the make-up, cologne, and perfume industry assumes that scents that are appealing to elk will also attract human males.

The prevailing science related to the notion of sexual attraction and olfactory stimulation revolves around the principles of DNA and, more specifically, major histocompatibility complex (MHC). Essentially, the basic genetic fact revolves around the idea that dominant (physiologically positive and, therefore, desirable) genetic traits are present in offspring over recessive (less positive and physiologically less healthy) genetic traits. This is why, simply stated, we don't mate with our siblings or other close, genetic relatives. With similar genetic profiles, brothers and sisters are more likely to share certain vulnerabilities that would become present in their children. Genetically speaking, opposites attract in the sense that good qualities are more likely to be fostered between two partners who are dissimilar.

Experiments that seek to determine the attraction and preference based upon scent have received recent attention. So called "T-shirt experiments" have plumbed this territory. In one such experiment conducted with nearly one hundred students at the University of Bern in Switzerland, the male students were asked to wear an untreated, cotton T-shirt to bed for two nights. The participants avoided deodorant, scented soaps, and spicy, odor-generating foods. After the two days of sweat infusion upon the T-shirts, the women participants were asked to respond to an exposure to the sampled shirts. Which shirt scents did they find appealing, and which did they find offensive? The general discovery and conclusion was that the female participants tended to be drawn to the shirts of males with dissimilar MHC profiles. Shirts they found offensive were typically from individuals with similar MHC backgrounds. In blind studies which replicated the T-shirt experimental design, biological relatives (fathers and brothers) were included in the sample population, and their shirts were also rejected by sisters and daughters.

So nature apparently has built into even evolved species, like we humans, protections against genetic disasters. On a physiological level, this is a positive. But for human females, there is more to a good partner than a desirable genetic profile. For the women of my research who attribute their past unsuccessful mate selections to unknown factors ("I honestly don't know why I was drawn to him. I just was."), pheromones may be the answer to that mystery. Finding a good, genetic mate is a good thing. (Let's not go back to the chromosomal disaster of inbreeding as practiced among royal families of European aristocracy.) Choosing a good partner should involve a rather dispassionate analysis of whom and why we are selecting certain individuals. Our earlier chapters were built around that premise.

While the women and girls who are the subject of this book will never be on trial for their ill-advised choice of partners, they will nevertheless suffer the sentence of the consequences of their poor relationship choices for a longer period of time than most convicts will. Their sentence will be to serve time in a loveless marriage, or endure a lifelong probation of being a single parent, raising children who will be the products of a divorce. Regrettably, in a culture that is rife with marital disintegration, these children will not be alone in either their lack of contact with a father, or their nomadic lifestyle of routinely bouncing from one residence to another as pawns of a joint custody decree.

Few would claim that breakups and divorce do not adversely impact both the marital partners and their off-spring. Most, however, essentially shrug their shoulders over such sad outcomes, believing that there is little that can be done about them. The lament is, "The heart wants what the heart wants." In other words, the heart is preem-inent over the brain; that emotions rule over logic. As a cognitive therapist, I would like to challenge this assump-tion, although I cannot deny that this is the existing cul-tural belief system.

Improving relationship choices will require a change in thinking. We need a new set of ideas about how we choose partners. An oft quoted line at AA meetings sug-gests, "Our best thinking has gotten us into the situation we find ourselves." The point clearly is that a change in life direction or, more specifically, a shift toward a more satisfying relationship direction, requires a change in our operational belief systems.

As a practicing clinician, I often share with clients my professional belief that everything about us flows from a few dominant, perhaps unconscious, beliefs. I may ask a client, as therapeutic homework, to ponder and write down what they consider to be their operational beliefs about themselves and others. Those four or five sentences, brought back into the next session, invariably prove instructive for me. More importantly, they are even more meaningful to the client who authored them.

Eric Berne, the creator of the theory of Transactional Analysis, refers to these dominant ideas as "script messages." Berne labels his concept of behavioral determination from the term we use for a playwright's creation: the script. Shakespeare tells us:

> All the world's a stage,
> And all the men and women merely players:
> They have their exits and their entrances;
> And one man in his time plays many parts…
>
> As You Like It 2:7

Berne suggests that we learn our "lines" during our childhood and, often, never stop to consider as adults the behaviors in which we engage. The lines we recite on a daily basis are, in fact, able to be changed. To give my readers a whimsical example that illustrates Berne's concept of scripting, imagine the following scenario. A woman has been cast in the role of the villainess in a community theatre production. Her character does many evil, vile things in the first act. In the middle of the second act, she is killed, much to the delight of the audience who

cheers at her demise. After the first weekend's performance, the actress who has just convincingly portrayed the
villainess approaches the play's director. She laments, "I
hate saying all those mean things in act one. It hurts my
feelings when everyone roars approval when I die in act
two. But since you're the director, I felt I needed to inform
you of my plans for next weekend's performances. Next
Friday, I'm not going to say or do anything bad in act one.
And I expect not to be murdered in act two. I'm going to
change my character's role completely."

What would any director do if confronted by such an
outrageous proclamation? None of us need to be experienced performers to predict that the director would give
his staff member two choices: either read the lines as written or get out of the play.

The great news, according to Eric Berne, is that in real
life there is a third choice. That choice is to re-write our
script. In other words, we can read the lines we have been
taught about ourselves, get out of the play (terminate the
behavior), or we can become a different person. That is,
we can re-write our script.

As children, we are scripted by our parents and other
influential adults with messages like, "You're shy." or,
"Why can't you be more like your sister?" or, "That's not
ladylike behavior." Sometimes the script messages can be
positive ones such as, "Connie's our little professor" or,
"Nobody is as persistent with something or works as hard
as Anita." For better or worse, as impressionable minors,
we take in these intonations, and they become a behavioral imprint that is difficult (but not impossible) to erase
or modify. They are subject to modification once we recognize and agree that we have the ability to make those
course corrections. While there are many different defini-

tions for what constitutes adulthood, my favorite definition of arriving at adulthood is when we reach the ability and requisite maturity to re-*write our script*.

So the point of this chapter is that while genetics and other biological factors do exist, we are able to overcome them. In Chapter 12, we will see how we can tap into our innate ability to make the correct (and rational) choice as it relates to choosing a partner.

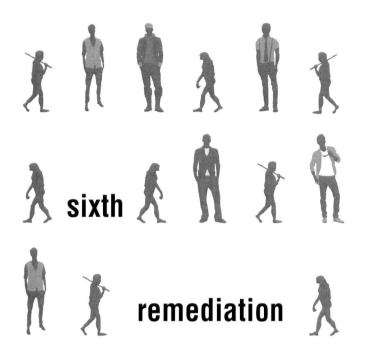

sixth

remediation

Disciplining yourself to do what you know is right
and important, although difficult, is the highroad to
pride, self-esteem, and personal satisfaction.

—Margaret Thatcher

Do the Right Thing!

One of my favorite movies is *Scent of a Woman*. I assume
that it is one of Al Pacino's favorites as well, as he won
the Academy Award as Best Actor for his portrayal of a
blind Army officer who befriends and, ultimately, defends
a young prep school boy who is being railroaded into
expulsion because of his refusal to inform on his miscreant

classmates. In the climatic scene that almost certainly won Pacino the Oscar, the blind Colonel Slade reflects on his life. In contrasting his own shortcomings with the courage and dignity exhibited by his mentee in refusing to rat on his friends, Colonel Slade ruefully observes, "Throughout my life, I always knew the correct thing to do. I knew it without exception. But I never did it. Why? Because it was too hard!"

That scene has always resonated with me, and the message conveyed in that short piece of dialogue. I believe that Pacino's character accurately expressed the reality of many of our experiences and life choices. Rarely, when we look back on past errors and misjudgments, were the mistakes due to a lack of knowledge or the inability to predict the outcome or response to a given statement or action. As we discussed in Chapter 4 (*linguini on the wall* reference), most outcomes are predictable. In other words, if I make a given remark, can I guess accurately as to the response I'm likely to receive? The answer is invariably yes. This naturally leads to the next question: Given that I'm not liking the response that I'm getting to what I just said (or did) and recognizing that the response I'm getting was predictable, why did I say what I just said (or do what I just did)?

If at this point readers are reflecting back on past failed statements or actions, and are feeling guilty or embarrassed or stupid about their role in their recalled relationship disaster, I counsel readers to stop there. Guilt is a conscience-driven but otherwise unproductive emotion. Guilt-oriented individuals *do guilt* in the way that some addicts do drugs. Instead, I am suggesting that the reader *do analysis* rather than *guilt*. It is far more productive to examine one's actions with the goal of correcting them than to feel guilty about them.

Many individuals from certain religious traditions are familiar with the concept of a guardian angel. The angel's primary function is to look after us, and assist us with moral or ethical decisions. It is the person's responsibility to listen to this "inner voice" and proceed accordingly.

I'm not certain if, in fact, we have such a mentor sitting on our shoulder like a virtue-spewing parrot, but I do think we have the psychological equivalent nevertheless. Some might label it as a conscience, although I believe this message-giver addresses issues that are more a function of sound judgment rather than moral imperatives. Others might consider this message-giver to be an inner voice. However it is identified, like Colonel Slade, I believe that the voice exists and would shape us into the direction of right action if we only choose to listen to it. I cannot claim knowledge as to its origins, but I can attest that it exists within all of the non-psychopathic population. (Psychopaths, by definition, are indifferent to issues of right and wrong. Either they are deaf to such moral input or merely choose to ignore those intonations.)

What does this little voice exist within non-psychopaths tell us exactly? It delivers two messages, I believe. The first message we have reviewed already; that we should act with right action. We should do the right thing. The other message, the quieter voice, delivers the perhaps more important message as it provides the energy, the fuel, for the ability to do the proper actions. That gentle voice is the soft whisper of hope. It is the feeling of well being that too often is covered by the suffocating effect of fear and doubt.

It has been said, in reference to spiritual belief, that if one wishes to have faith, then she should act as if she has faith and faith will be given to her. This principle applies to hope as well. It is important for all women to come to the belief that there is hope for a better life, for a more balanced and fulfilling relationship. As my readers have progressed through the first six chapters of this book, many will have come to reach an understanding of their own tendencies with respect to relationships. They recognize the signs of low self-esteem, or a need to be a helper, or to control, or seek *excitement*, or to be cared for. This insight will be useful only if it is married to hope, however.

Hope
Hope is the feathered thing
That perches in the soul,
And sings the tune—without the words,
And never stops at all.

—Emily Dickinson

As I explained the metaphor of the snowman earlier in this work, you will recall that it represents my basic approach to counseling. My theoretical orientation suggests that our thoughts lead to our behaviors and, in turn, our behaviors lead to feelings, positive or negative. In other words, all of our actions flow from some idea or belief. Personal beliefs, therefore, dictate future actions. When we apply this principle to the business of partner choice, we can understand that every woman must learn to accept and believe that she can change. Hope is the requisite commodity that will allow women to move forward. Hope for change is the polar opposite to the irrational, destructive notion, "This is just the way I am."

In an earlier chapter, I challenged the readers of this book to engage in the potentially unsettling exercise of staring into a mirror for a solid sixty seconds. I cautioned that this activity would not be as simple as it sounds. "Do the right thing" mandates a course of action that is as psychologically daunting as our mirror exercise. I invite my readers to submit to the exercise and share the results with me on my website (snowmantherapy.com). Simply put, I challenge the readers of this work to set aside their distracting thoughts, fears, and perceived inadequacies and do the right thing. Not the safe thing; not the popular thing; and not the convenient thing. Look into the metaphorical mirror, and *do the right thing*.

As we apply this exercise back to the capable, female readers of this book who have a history of unsatisfying relationships, there is challenging but insightful information flowing to them through the reflective glass. Their image may be telling them that they need to feel better about themselves; that whatever the basis of their negative sense of themselves may be, it is time to reject those self-defeating personal evaluations (the *low self-esteem* strand). Or their reflection may be telling them that they have a troubling tendency to be dictatorial or pedantic; that they unconsciously have chosen ineffectual partners that they can dominate and, later, resent for their lack of spine or initiative (1 *control* strand). And so on.

The point is that the answer is truly in the looking glass. It is within us, if we choose to see. But moving from insight to action requires courage. Thinking comes easier than acting. We are now considering the vital link to courage. As we discussed earlier, courage is not fearlessness. Rather, it is action in the face of fear.

But while we are acting with courage, it is equally important to proceed from a hopeful, optimistic point of view. As you move forward with the daunting looking glass exercise, allow yourself to generate a little smile as you recognize that you are, in fact, OK. You are a good person who may have made poor choices in the past but are now moving forward toward better choices and a better life.

Now look into the mirror. See. Think. Smile. Then act. Do the right thing.

> Good decisions come from experience, and
> experience comes from bad decisions.
>
> —Anonymous

concluding remarks

Hopefully, the preceding twelve chapters generated some insights for those women who have chosen to persevere through its pages. If it has been helpful, that probably means that it was somewhat painful at times as well. My students and clients would probably agree that their professor or their therapist is a font of one-liners, and I must plead guilty to that observation. One of those commonly expressed aphorisms is: "Nobody changes in the midst of a positive situation." While most of us would like to think of ourselves as intelligent and analytical, the truth is that the majority tends to bump along with the same set of behaviors and habits until something (or somebody) pushes us in another direction. The agent of change might be a judge, or a boss, or a spouse, or our physician, but no one ever makes a significant change in course direction without some source of human energy pushing us to adjust our conduct. Or to use another example from the opposite direction, picture the following:

> A person (man or woman) awakens on a Thursday morning considering life. Self-talk summarizes, "I love my spouse and family. I have a terrific job and a good boss. I just passed my physical with high marks from my doctor. I've never been arrested for anything more serious than a parking ticket. But I drink too much."

What would ever lead this hypothetical individual to arrive at such a conclusion? In over twenty-five years as a practicing clinician, I have never had a client who presented him/herself for help with such a narrative. Clients seek change because something bad or unsatisfying is presenting itself. They were busted for drinking and driving. Or their spouse threatened to get a lawyer if they didn't straighten up. Or their employer referred them to the company's EAP (Employee Assistance Program) because of their attendance or work-performance issues. Or their doctor expressed concern about their blood pressure or liver count. Simply stated: no one leaps into counseling. They get pushed by life's circumstances. And that's okay.

I hope that this book provided a loving shove for you. Earlier, I mentioned that I teach my students, future clinicians, that we are not advisors. Rather, we are professional mirror holders. I invite my readers to look one last time into that mirror by considering the following final bromide:

> Life is all about going against our tendencies.

Our tendencies are simply our patterns of behavior. Perhaps they are genetically influenced. Maybe they are all learned. No matter. They are roadmaps that steer our course through life. And all of our tendencies fall into two categories: they are either positive tendencies or negative ones.

It is easy to know what to do about our negative tendencies. Whether we incline toward procrastination or greasy French fries, we know that these tendencies should be changed or avoided. We may struggle in attempting to do so, but we never lack for an understanding of what right action is. No student sitting on a couch when she should be studying for tomorrow's exam is confused about the appropriateness of her lethargy. And no New Year's resolution to lose weight was broken in the drive-thru of the fast food restaurant out of the erroneous belief that supersizing meant more of a good thing. We always have a clear understanding of our bad tendencies.

Our good tendencies are trickier to address because they are just that: good tendencies. A tendency to be thrifty would generally be considered to be a good quality, for example. But an individual who wishes to purchase a home but is reluctant to take out a mortgage is missing an opportunity in 2012 to buy in a depressed housing market, especially with record low interest rates. To refer back to my research and the strands of this book, there is no more admirable or stereotypically positive feminine quality than the desire to nurture. But as we described earlier, it can be a prelude to a relationship disaster. So risk takers should demonstrate more caution, and the cautious should lean toward bolder strokes.

Progress in life is all about recognizing, then going against, our tendencies when wisdom and self-understanding dictates the more prudent, but also courageous, course. The poet Homer tells us:

The journey is the thing

Enjoy yours.

introduction to questionnaire

Enclosed you will find a questionnaire that is aimed at exploring a certain type of relationship. As both a clinician and an educator, it has been my experience that capable, talented, and generally functional women often attach themselves to males who are seemingly far less capable or achieving. It is also my observation that the reverse situation (capable men with dysfunctional women) occurs far less often.

Why is this? That is the question that my research, and this questionnaire, seeks to explore.

I am asking for your help in one of two ways. First, if you have ever been (or are) in such a relationship, please complete the enclosed. Second, if you know of a woman (a friend, or relative, or co-worker) who has experienced such a dysfunctional relationship, please pass this survey on to her.

If you'd like to discuss this further, you can provide your name and a phone number or email address here:

_____

_____

Thanks for your help and cooperation.

—Dr. John V. Farrar
drjohn@snowmantherapy.com

questionnaire

If you need more room for any question, please use the opposite page, and place the number of the question you are answering before the response.

1 Your age _____

2 Have you ever been in a relationship that you considered unfulfilling that lasted longer than three months? Yes_____ No _____ How many relationships?_____

3 How long were you in/have you been in this relationship?
    _____

4 Indicate your most current level of academic achievement by circling one of the following:

Some high school	Bachelors degree
High school graduate	Master's degree
Some college	Post master's

5 Have you ever been in trouble with the law? Explain.
    _____
    _____

6 Has the partner from that relationship partner ever been in trouble with the law? Explain. _____
    _____
    _____

7   Are you the only, oldest, youngest, or middle child in your family? _____

8   Is/was that partner the only, oldest, youngest, or middle child in his family?_____ Explain.

_____

_____

9   Choose the option which best describes your role when you lived with your parent(s)/guardian(s):

• Parents were largely responsible for the household and care for your siblings.

• You helped out somewhat but let your parents handle the majority of the workload.

• You helped out around the house often, under the direction of your parent/s.

• You were largely responsible for care of the household and care of younger siblings.

10 On a scale of 1 to 10 (10 being the highest), how would you rate your self-esteem? _____

11 Choose the one that best describes you:

• Your self-esteem is higher than the level of others in your peer group.

• Your self-esteem seems to be lower than that of others in you peer group.

• Your self-esteem is at the same level as your friends.

12 Do you feel that your self-esteem has been enhanced by this relationship or diminished by it? _____

13 Do/did your friends often tell you that you could do so much better than the male you are with?_____

_____

14 Do you feel you could do/have done better? _____
Why or why not? _____

_____

_____

15 Why were you first attracted to this partner? _____

_____

_____

17 What do/did you like most about his personality?

_____

_____

_____

18 Describe how you feel/felt about yourself when you are/were with him:_____

_____

_____

19 Has his personality changed over the course of the relationship? Describe._____

_____

_____

20 Do/did your parents like your partner? Why or why not? _____

_____

_____

21 Do/did his parents like you? Why or why not?_____

_____

_____

22 Is/was your relationship emotionally satisfying for you? (Are/were your emotional needs met?) _____

If no, why not? _____
_____

If no, explain your reasons for staying in the relationship.
_____
_____

If yes, how/why? _____
_____
_____

23 Has your partner ever been physically or emotionally abusive with you? _____ If yes, explain. ____
_____
_____

If yes, does/did he promise to change after the abusive act? _____

24 How many times did you break up? _____

When you did get back together, what led to the reconciliation?_____
_____
_____

25 If you are broken up right now, and your partner were to attempt to re-establish the relationship, what would you do? Explain._____
_____
_____

26 Are/were you afraid that you will lose touch with certain friends if you and your partner were to break up/separate/divorce? _____

27 What three words would describe your feelings at the beginning of the relationship?_____,
_____, and _____

28 What three words would describe your feelings in the final few weeks of the relationship? _____, _____, and _____

29 If you are no longer in the relationship, as you look back on it, what did you learn or how have you changed as a result of it?_____

_____

_____

30 Are you currently in a new relationship? _____

31 If yes, which term best describes your new relationship in comparison to the one you have described earlier in the survey?

a better   c worse

b same   d uncertain

Why? _____

_____

_____

motivation questionnaire

Research conducted thus far suggests that there exists certain themes or strands that are linked to the type of relationships this study is investigating. They are listed below along with a space to include your own strand that may not be included in the other choices. These themes or strands seek to determine what a female's motivations are for entering and remaining in such a relationship.

Please attempt to account for your past relationship by assigning a percentage value to the themes that contributed to the relationship. For example, a respondent may account for a prior relationship this way:

Self-esteem issues	=	50%	This breakdown implies
Nurturing issues	=	50%	that this woman lacked
Excitement issues	=	0%	a positive self image and
Control issues	=	0%	also enjoyed the role of
Chemistry	=	0%	caretaking her partner.
Being nurtured	=	0%	
Total	=	100%	

Self-esteem issues   =   0%
Nurturing issues   =   0%
Excitement issues   =   60%
Control issues   =   0%
Chemistry   =   40%
Being nurtured   =   0%

Total   =   100%

This woman's initial motivations were based on a conscious desire for a stimulating relationship (*excitement* issues) along with being attracted to this partner for reasons that were not clearly understood (*chemistry*).

Issues

Self-esteem issues (feeling less confident or unworthy of a better partner) _____ %

Nurturing issues (feeling good about caring for another) _____ %

Excitement issues (Some males involved in less conventional behavior and lifestyles are more interesting than males with conventional lifestyles.) _____ %

Control issues (feeling able to manage a relationship rather than being managed by a stronger partner) _____ %

Chemistry (feeling attracted without consciously knowing why) _____ %

Desire to be nurtured (feeling protected and cared for) _____ %

Other (describe briefly) _____ %

Total (must equal 100%) _____ %

winning women's personality profile

Would you describe your parents as critical or nurturing?

Critical _____   Nurturing _____

Would you describe yourself as self-reliant or helpful to others?

Self-reliant _____   Helpful _____

I wouldn't want to be in a relationship where my partner earned more than I.

True _____   False _____

I tend to choose older partners.

True _____   False _____

I like to gamble.

True _____   False _____

I honestly don't know why I've chosen some of my past partners.

True _____   False _____

Were you ever compared unfavorably to siblings or other children?

Yes _____   No _____

I am currently in (or plan to enter) a helping profession (i.e. teaching, nursing, social work, counseling, etc.)

True _____   False _____

In groups, I often end up in a leadership role.

True _____ False _____

I tend to avoid leadership roles.

True _____ False _____

I'm easily bored.

True _____ False _____

I'm often attracted to individuals who I don't consider to be physically attractive or interesting in some way.

True _____ False _____

I am basically dissatisfied with my physical appearance.

True _____ False _____

One of my greatest joys is in helping others.

True _____ False _____

I'm critical (at least in my own mind) of individuals who demonstrate negative addictions.

True _____ False _____

I like it when others help me with problems or difficult situations.

True _____ False _____

I enjoy high adventure movies and entertainment events.

True _____ False _____

I often feel drawn to certain people for no clear reason.

True _____ False _____

Do you wish you had more friends?

Yes _____ No _____

I find attractive, confident members of the opposite sex (or same sex) strangely unappealing or intimidating.

True _____ False _____

I prefer younger partners.

> True _____   False _____

I am an attention seeker.

> True _____   False _____

I consider myself to be physically active.

> True _____   False _____

My friends often question my choice of partners, and I do too.

> True _____   False _____

Would you describe yourself as a follower or a leader?

> Leader _____   Follower _____

I feel happiest when I feel I am contributing to a greater good.

> True _____   False _____

I generally feel I know the best course of action in a work situation.

> True _____   False _____

I was the youngest child (but not an only child) in my family.

> True _____   False _____

I tend to choose unpredictable, adventurous partners rather than stable, conventional ones.

> True _____   False _____

I seem to make a connection with some people for no apparent reason.

> True _____   False _____

Are you comfortable with alone time?

> Yes _____   No _____

I am a people person.

> True _____   False _____

My mother tended to wear the pants in my family of origin.

True _____   False _____

I consider myself to be quiet rather than outgoing.

True _____   False _____

I think people who present themselves in unusual ways (i.e. tattoos, piercing, unconventional attire) are attractive.

True _____   False _____

I seemingly had little in common with some of my previous partners.

True _____   False _____

It is very important to me to be part of the group.

True _____   False _____

People usually turn to me for favors or assistance with something.

True _____   False _____

I dislike gambling or risky investments.

True _____   False _____

I had an unsatisfactory or absent relationship with my father.

True _____   False _____

I find traditional values to be outmoded or restricting.

True _____   False _____

I believe in fate or karma.

True _____   False _____

Did you consider yourself to be an underachiever in school or in your career?

Yes_____   No_____

Do you often end up rescuing others in the midst of problems?

Yes_____   No_____

I'd rather work independently on a project than function within a group.

True _____   False_____

I seem to attract people who look after me.

True _____   False_____

I consider myself to be a conservative person.

True _____   False_____

At times I feel a connection to some individuals that doesn't seem logical.

True _____   False_____

I value any form of acknowledgement, praise, or recognition.

True _____   False_____

If I decided to choose a pet from the Humane Society, I'd tend to pick the one that needed adopting rather than the most attractive or healthiest dog (cat).

True _____   False_____

I'm comfortable taking an opposite position in a discussion.

True _____   False_____

I generally let others (including my partners) make important decisions.

True _____   False_____

I consider partners who generally give me my way to be weak or uninteresting.

True _____   False_____

I believe that there are biological factors (rather than looks or personality) that contribute to whom we choose as a partner.

    True _____   False _____

I tend to blame myself when being mistreated or discounted or abused.

    True _____   False _____

I believe that a good woman puts the needs of others ahead of her own needs.

    True _____   False _____

I like to win; it's important to me.

    True _____   False _____

I often end up in situations in which others rescue me.

    True _____   False _____

I find guys who keep you guessing to be stimulating and a challenge.

    True _____   False _____

I do believe that there is such a thing as animal magnetism for humans.

    True _____   False _____

After completing this profile, email to drjohn@snowman-therapy.com to have it scored and returned to you.

questionnaire response statistics

Statistics below are based upon 259 respondents who completed the survey fully.

Average (mean) age of the respondents: 31.8 years

	Low Self-Esteem	Nurturing	Excitement
% identifying strand as factor	59.4%	78.6%	56.7%
% identifying strand as most important factor	36%	16%	10%
% identifying this strands as sole factor	.4% (1 total)	.8% (2 total)	0%

	Control	Desire to be nurtured	Chemistry
% identifying strand as factor	29.7%	51.3%	78.3%
% identifying strand as most important factor	12 %	12%	14%
% identifying this strands as sole factor	0%	0%	0%

Questionnaire Findings and Observations:

- The most commonly mentioned factors (but not necessarily the most important factor) were *nurturing* and *chemistry* (78%).

- *Low self-esteem* was cited as the single *most important* factor in their poor mate selection by 36% of the respondents.

- Women who cited *control* issues as a factor in their relationship choice tended to be older (Average age of 37.6 years).

- Women who cited *excitement* as a factor tended to be younger (Average age of 25.1 years).

- There was a very high positive correlation between women who identified as having *low self* esteem and their tendency to be *nurturers* (86%).

- Only three women of the 259 respondents listed *only one strand* as the reason for their relationship choice.

- A surprisingly low percent of oldest children cited *control* as a factor in their relationship choice. (21.6%)

- A surprisingly high percent of middle children listed *desire to be nurtured* as a factor in their relationship choice (76.9%). This contrasts with a figure of only 51.3% for the respondents surveyed.

bibliography

Adler, A. (1956). *The Individual Psychology of Alfred Adler.* H. L. Ansbacher and R. R. Ansbacher (Eds.). New York: Harper Torchbooks

Beck, A.T. *Cognitive Therapy and the Emotional Disorders.* Intl Universities Press, 1975.

Berne, Eric. *Games People Play: The Psychology of Human Relationships.* New York: Ballantine, 1973.

Carenegie, Dale. *How to Win Friends & Influence People.* New York: Simon & Schuster, revised 1981.

Forward, Susan Ph.D. & Joan Torres. *Men Who Hate Women and the Women who Love Them.* New York: Bantam Books 2002.

Gilligan, Carol. "Mapping the Moral Domain: A Contribution of Women's Thinking to Psychological Theory and Education," Harvard University Press, 1989.

Glasser, William. *Choice Theory: A New Psychology of Personal Freedom.* New York: Harper Collins, 1998.

Gottman, John. *Why Marriages Succeed or Fail: and How You Can Make Yours Last.* New York: Simon & Schuster, 1994.

Gray, John Ph.D. *Men are from Mars, Women are From Venus.* New York: Harper Collins, 1995.

Harris, Thomas. *I'm OK, You're OK.* Harper 2004.

Jacobellis v. Ohio, 378 U.S. 184, 197 (1964).

Luft, J.; Ingham, H. "The Johari Window, a graphic model of interpersonal awareness." *Proceedings of the western training laboratory in group development* (Los Angeles: UCLA), 1955.

Luft, Joseph. *Of Human Interaction.* Palo Alto, CA: National Press, 1969.

Meyers, Isabel Briggs. *Myers–Briggs Type Indicator,* Palo Alto, CA: Consulting Psychologists Press, Inc. 1985.

Rotter, J. B. *Social Learning and Clinical Psychology.* New York: Prentice-Hall, 1954.

Seligman, Martin. *Optimistic Child.* Massachusetts: Houghton Mifflin Harcourt, 2007.

Seligman, Martin E. P. (2004). "Can Happiness be Taught?" *Daedalus*, Spring 2004.

Spock, Benjamin. Baby and Child Care. (7th ed.) New York City: Pocket Books, 1998.

Sternberg, Robert J. (1988). *The Triangle of Love: Intimacy, Passion,* Commitment. New York: Basic Books.

Watson, John B. *Behaviorism* (revised edition). University of Chicago Press, 1930.

Weiner, B. *Human Motivation: Metaphors, Theories, and Research.* Sage Publications, 1992.

In memory of my mot'

Mary Anne L

who surrendered '
to borrow money for

Live
Like
Louis!

Inspiring Stories
From the Life
Of Louis Armstrong
To Help You Lead
A More *Wonderful* Life

Phil Lynch

16th Street Press

Bach said everything is in its place;
Armstrong said the sun comes shining through.

- Richard Brookhiser

Program

Live
Like
Louis!

Intro

*in which you and I become acquainted
and begin at the end of Louis's life*

I invite you to close your eyes and think of Louis Armstrong. What comes to mind? If you picture something, I'll bet it's Satchmo's huge smile. He was indeed a happy man who enjoyed life with a very positive outlook. When you think of Louis, do you hear anything? Maybe you can hear his boisterous laugh or that warm, gravelly voice singing "What a Wonderful World," the song that has become his anthem of sorts. It's an appropriate one for him, since it pretty much summarizes his actual outlook on life. As a musician, when I call him to mind, I hear his lively early jazz playing that established him as a great soloist and the founding father of "swing."

There are many facets to Louis Armstrong: jazz icon, innovative singer, "pop" crossover artist, radio and movie star, globetrotting jazz ambassador, and non-stop professional musician who toured almost to his dying day. And of course there's Louis Armstrong, the man. Whenever I would tell someone I was writing about Louis, literally each person would smile and say something positive about Louis or one of his songs. Even my high school students, even *they* feel positively about him, and they're "cool" teenagers! Years ago I was in the church business and someone advised me that you can talk about religion or your beliefs and really turn some people off. But talk about Jesus and pretty much everybody still likes *him*. I've found the same thing true with Louis: seriously, who dislikes Louis Armstrong? Moreover, a number of events and individuals in his fascinating life can serve to inspire us to be better people ourselves.

If you're not really into jazz or music history, you can rest easy: this isn't a book about music. It's a book about living. Someone once asked Louis if jazz was folk music. He replied, "All music is folk music. I ain't never heard no horse sing a song." I intend this book not for jazz fans or music buffs, but for folks, for anyone who can use a little inspiration to be a better person. If that's you (and I hope it is), I invite you to come along as we explore stories and people from the life of Louis Armstrong. I'll be careful not to give advice; I won't say, "Just do thus and such." I think it works better to offer reminders and examples of how we *can* be. So at the end of each chapter, you'll find personal growth practices to try if you wish. There are also suggested songs to listen to, with links available on the companion website, www.livelikelouis.com.

One of leadership expert Stephen Covey's famous seven habits of effective people is to begin with the end in mind. So, before we begin in chap-

ter one to contemplate the difficult early surroundings Louis overcame, it's important we share an
understanding of what he did with his life.

Accomplishments

I thought I knew "Pops" (the name his friends
called him) pretty well. But while researching his
life, I was really impressed by how "far out" Louis
Armstrong really was. Or is. You see, he's still far
out today, literally out of this world: one of his early
recordings is on the Voyager spacecraft now leaving our solar system! I can think of no better repre-
sentative of the human race. Some alien "cats" will
be "diggin' ol' Satch" light years away some day.

But seriously, let's hear what experts have to
say about Louis. *Time* named him one of its 100
most important people of the 20th century. That's
people in general, not just entertainers. Filmmaker
Ken Burns says, "Armstrong is to music what Ein-
stein is to physics and the Wright Brothers are to
travel." Gary Giddins, one of our best music critics,
calls Armstrong "America's Bach." Duke Ellington,
whom many would nominate as America's greatest
composer, simply called Louis "Mister Jazz." Tony
Bennett (himself a U.N. Citizen of the World) says,
"The bottom line of any country in the world is
'What did we contribute to the world?' We contributed Louis Armstrong."

Halls of fame really like Louis. He's in at least
eight including the Rock and Roll Hall of Fame (for
his influence on the blues). That same hall includes

his "West End Blues" as one of its 500 most influential recordings. Eleven of his records are in the Grammy Hall of Fame, and he won the Grammy Lifetime Achievement Award posthumously. Naturally, Louis has a star on that famous sidewalk in Hollywood.

Let's move back in time a bit. At Louis's passing in 1971, both the president and State Department issued public statements of condolence. Louis's honorary pallbearers included the governor of New York, the mayor of New York City, the aforementioned Duke of Ellington, plus Bing Crosby, Frank Sinatra, and Johnny Carson. At the time of his passing, Louis had played hundreds of dates a year for almost thirty years, including one in Ghana attended by 100,000 people. He had made countless TV appearances, been in over thirty films, and officially represented his country on three foreign continents. Always traveling with a typewriter, he had written two autobiographies. He was the first black man to have a national radio show.

Musically, he wrote dozens of songs and put many others on the map. He transformed singing by being the first to sing songs as freely as a jazz instrumentalist would play them. He would still sing the lyrics (mostly), but alter the rhythm and change the tune. He was improvising, in other words, and no one on record had sung like that before. Tony Bennett believes

> Armstrong practically invented jazz singing and was the greatest influence not only in jazz, but for all music. . . . Armstrong influ-

enced Billie Holiday, Sinatra, everybody. To this day in the music business . . . you'll find Armstrong got there first.

Bing Crosby said, "Do you realize that the greatest pop singer that ever was and ever will be forever and ever is Louis Armstrong?"

In addition to singing lyrics more freely, he pioneered "scat singing": eliminating the lyrics altogether and singing nonsense syllables. Imitating a horn, in other words. It's a staple of jazz singing now, made famous by greats like Ella Fitzgerald and Mel Tormé. Louis wasn't quite the first to do it on record, though he might have been the first to do it in an improvised (spur-of-the-moment) way. Regardless, he put scat singing on the map with one huge hit record that even changed how people spoke in Chicago.

If this weren't enough, Louis Armstrong changed how the trumpet was played, exploring with his high notes where no trumpeter had gone before. Early on, both jazz and classical players liked to examine his horn, expecting to find a trick trumpet. Each time, they discovered the magic was not in the horn, but in the man. Dizzy Gillespie, who took trumpeting to even greater heights in the 1940s and '50s said simply, "Without him, no me." Trumpeter Miles Davis pioneered several distinct styles of jazz and remarked, "You can't play anything on a horn that Louis hasn't played."

One last thing: in the 1920s he merely changed what jazz essentially was and established what it then would be. As a soloist in others' bands, he set the bar both for virtuosity and a relaxed, swinging feel. Then with the records he made with his own small combos, he established jazz as a music for soloists rather than the more collaborative, ensemble style it was before. Instead of B.C. and A.D., it wouldn't be at all unreasonable to date music history B.A. and A.A., if you know what I mean.

Jazz founder. Trumpet virtuoso. Pioneering vocalist. Jazz/pop crossover artist. Radio, movie, and TV star. Musical ambassador. International icon. And most importantly, a man who lived with the purpose of bringing joy to others and leaving the world better than he found it. His purpose and way of living are much harder to quantify than accolades and achievements, but ultimately far more important. As Duke Ellington put it, Louis was "born poor, died rich, and never hurt anyone along the way." As an educator, I'm not going to end up with one of my lesson plans onboard a spacecraft or be nominated to the Teaching Hall of Fame. I can, however, learn from the way Louis lived and be a better human being through his example. So in the pages to come, we'll explore ten aspects of living well, such as encouraging others, building on your strengths, showing courage, and living out a sense of purpose.

As we begin the first chapter, keep in mind Louis's accomplishments and the positive way he lived his life. Because now we're traveling back to the beginning, to appreciate the magnitude of the journey Louis Armstrong took. The man who died beloved by millions was born in a battlefield.

Listening Suggestions

Links to audio and video files are found at
www.livelikelouis.com.

Let's save trumpet virtuosity and scat singing for other chapters and focus here on how Louis improvised. That is, how he spontaneously created new tunes and rhythms.

It's impossible to hear Louis Armstrong now as people heard him in the 1920s and '30s when he was musically going where no "cat" had gone before. It's hard to hear how he's altering a tune or rhythm if we're not familiar with the "straight" (normal) version. Granted, the "standard" songs recorded by many artists over the years have had a resurgence lately, thanks to artists like Rod Stewart, Carly Simon, and Michael Bublé. Still, we're often unaware of the straight versions of Louis's songs, to appreciate how masterfully he changed them.

Of the songs Louis recorded in his most energetic years, "Georgia on My Mind" probably has the best chance of being known by us post-moderns, thanks to Ray Charles. Satchmo begins with eight measures played pretty straight; but he's already altering things a bit in the next eight bars. Sixteen measures of violins and syrupy saxes bring us to Louis's vocal treatment of the song. Listen to a masterful singer improvise, altering the song's tune and rhythm, though the melody is still close by. Then listen to the then-unequalled master of the trumpet improvise on his horn.

During his trumpet solo he'll even throw in a two-measure quote from "Rhapsody in Blue" for you, if you know that piece. Louis established jazz as a soloist's art and was the first player in modern times to show how improvisers could be just as beautifully imaginative as composers who write down their notes. In fact, jazz artists are composing a new melody each time they solo – and in front of an audience. No pressure there, eh?

There's another song by Hoagie Carmichael many of us still might know. It's "Stardust," of which *Wikipedia* presently says there are 1,800 recordings. Listen to Louis's 1931 recording. Most jazz artists will play a melody pretty straight the first time, with minimal changes. But right out of the blocks, King Louis is wonderfully altering an already-beautiful melody, though it's still recognizable. After he plays one chorus, he enters singing the same note repeatedly. Then he takes off. Groundbreaking. And just as important, joyful.

1 Don't Fence Me In

*in which Louis shows us
we can rise above our circumstances*

It wasn't just any battlefield Louis was born in, it was "The Battlefield," a poor black neighborhood in turn-of-the-century New Orleans. Try to imagine it in 1906: houses are closely packed, with outhouses in the back. Horses fill the streets, and the humid air is heavy with odors. The cries of street vendors are heard. The children are barefoot. One of them, a five-year-old boy, is returning from a cistern. He carries water for his caretaker grandmother. But when he arrives back at her small house, a mysterious old woman is with her; both wear serious expressions. The stranger says the boy is to leave the only home he has known and go with her. He must care for his sick mother.

His grandmother dresses him in the better of his two sets of clothing. "I really hate to let you out of my sight," she sighs. But as Louis would write in his memoirs five decades later, his grandmother is a "grand person" and doesn't think twice about parting with the boy so that his mother could be cared for. His touching reply, recollected fifty years later, shows how he treasured his grandmother:

> I am sorry to leave you too Granny. . . .You have been so kind and so nice to me, taught me everything I know: how to take care of myself, how to wash myself and brush my teeth, put my clothes away, mind the older folks.

Then his hand is taken by the stranger and he is led away. When they turn the corner and he can no longer see his grandmother, the boy naturally starts to cry. They wait for the trolley, in front of the House of Detention. The woman tells the five-year-old she'll have him sent there if he doesn't stop bawling. He takes her at her word. The streetcar arrives and, never having ridden one, the boy goes right to the front to get a good view. But this is 1906 in New Orleans, the city where Homer Plessy sued all the way to the Supreme Court to get railway cars desegregated. And lost. "Separate but equal" is the law of the land, and the boy cannot read the very large sign specifying where not to sit. The thrill of being on a streetcar has overcome his sorrow for a time and he is "acting cute" in the front.

The woman motions to the boy to come to the back of the trolley. He ignores her. She storms up and drags the "little fool" to the back. They ride for several minutes to the Back o' Town neighborhood near Liberty and Perdido streets, then walk two blocks to a room facing a back courtyard. There they find a very sick twenty-year-old woman on a pallet. It is Louis's mother and it is now his job to take care of her.

Louis's Upbringing

This key moment in Louis's life illustrates his childhood and what he overcame. It is also very telling about his adult life, because what we know of this episode comes from recollections written in his fifties. The gratitude he expresses to his grandmother in his 1954 memoir exemplifies the gratitude he generally expressed throughout his life for a great many people and things, even events in his childhood most would consider bad. Also, the event on the trolley shows him literally crossing the boundary between white and black. Later he would be the first black star embraced by whites, who would come to enjoy him more than fellow blacks did. Nevertheless, dealing with racism was a fact of life for any black man, whether entertainer or bricklayer. We'll explore these themes in later chapters. Let's examine Louis's childhood circumstances a bit more.

He was born to a fifteen-year-old mother and twenty-year-old father who weren't married and had an on-and-off sort of relationship. His mother gave birth in 1901 in his grandmother's house in the aforementioned "Battlefield" neighborhood of New Orleans. It was named the Battlefield because – why else? – it was the scene of considerable chaos and fighting. In fact, it was the black red-light district. Young Louis's neighbors were gamblers, thieves,

pimps, and prostitutes, with some ordinary working stiffs mixed in: Louis's father worked at a tur-
pentine factory until his death in 1933. But his parents split up shortly after his birth and both moved
out after he was born, leaving him with his grandmother. Louis occasionally would see his father
marching in parades, and would later write of the
pride he had for the man and his skills in strutting.
But aside from a brief stay with him as a teen, Louis
had no real relationship with his father.

Louis's mother, Mayann, did indeed get well after he arrived to take care of her. Louis had a number of "stepfathers" (his mother's live-in boyfriends) who varied in their treatment of Mayann,
Louis, and his little sister. Satchmo's biographers
believe that at least occasionally Mayann prosti-
tuted herself, which would not have been uncom-
mon for a single woman with children to support.
Louis went to school though he was always working too, selling papers. He dropped out of the fifth
grade when he was eleven years old and began
singing for coins in a street quartet. (If you're ever
at the Superdome, cross Poydras Street at Freret,
and you can hang out on the corner where Pops
first performed.) Like other boys attracted to illicit
goings-on, he would linger outside rough honky-
tonks like the "Funky Butt," peeking through cracks
in the boards; or sneak into "Dago Tony's" and hide
behind the piano to be near the musicians.

Then on New Year's Eve, 1912, Louis Armstrong fired a gun in the air and was sent to a reformatory, the Colored Waif's Home. After a year
and a half, Louis was reluctant to leave that disci-

plined environment but was released nevertheless. He ended up with his father's second family for a time. Due to sibling troubles and his father's inability to provide, however, he returned to his mother and sister and helped support them, staying with them until leaving home in 1919. His mother took in laundry, they had no bathroom, and all shared one bed. Louis described the family as poor but "clean," and remarked in his 1954 memoir that all types of people treated Mayann with respect, and she in turn "always held her head up."

Louis then worked on a wagon delivering coal to prostitutes in Storyville, New Orleans' storied red-light district. On Saturday mornings he could sell buckets of brick dust to the working women there. They thought it good luck to sprinkle it on the walk after scrubbing the front steps with their urine. I can't attest to whether it actually brought them luck, but it stands as an example of what young Louis saw while growing up.

If we translated this to the twenty-first century, we really wouldn't have to change many of the details. A son with an absent father drops out of school, takes to the streets, commits a crime, does some time, gets out. What comes next? More jail time, right? After an initial lock up, it's likely in and out of jail or prison. There is little to show when death comes, probably at a young age through violence or substance abuse. I witnessed this pattern firsthand in a cheerful student of mine after he did time in a nearby juvenile lockup for stealing a van. He returned a different person, sullen, tough, and thinking himself a criminal. Having

14   *Live Like Louis!*

a rusted gun in his locker got him expelled, and so the cycle continued.

Future offenses and incarceration would be an accurate prediction in a lot of cases. But not always. And not in Louis's case. Remember his lifetime accomplishments? Plus all the joy he brought to his listeners? Clearly his rugged surroundings and early experiences did not define or confine him.

No Victim of Circumstances

Another star of the 1930s, Mr. Jerome Howard, used a certain line in many of his short films. He'd be surrounded by plumbing, or have a lobster stuck to his nose, with his brother about to slap him. Wanting to escape the inevitable, he'd plead, "I'm just a victim of 'coicumstance'!" You might know Jerome better by his stage name, Curly, of the Three Stooges. And if you've seen a Stooges film, I'm sure you can hear his high-pitched voice making that claim (probably followed by a couple of "nyuk-nyuks" and the slap from Moe).

Unlike Curly, however, Louis Armstrong – though raised in abject poverty and surrounded by crime and substance abuse – never claimed to be a victim of circumstance. His very challenging circumstances did not define him, just as your circumstances do not have to define you; neither the situation when you were young nor your situation now. This is an old truth, as most truths are. But it bears hearing again.

Certainly, Louis's circumstances did influence

him. This is inescapable. We're always being influenced by everything around us. Some fascinating
research placed people in a room where the Apple
Computer logo was subtly displayed; others were
in a room with the IBM logo. Which people performed more creatively? I don't even have to tell
you, do I? We've been pummeled for years by ads
telling us PC is boring and Mac is cool. Just their
logos affected people's behavior without their even
knowing. In a similar experiment, people were assigned to a room with either the Disney logo or the
E Entertainment Network logo. One group responded to questions more truthfully. Guess which
group. (Hint: it wasn't the group seeing the logo we
associate with celebrity dirt and gossip.)

And if logos influence us, how much more so
do *people*? Famous research by Solomon Asch in the
1950s placed one person among a group. Everyone
else in the group was "in" on the experiment. These
undercover participants would discuss three lines
on a paper and come to a very wrong group decision on which two were the same length. Asch observed that when three others agreed on a wrong
answer, the unknowing individual would often go
along with that obviously wrong group statement,
although he or she knew it to be false. And history
shows us that even a whole nation can take a terrible wrong turn as neighbor reinforces neighbor in
some horrific belief or attitude. We must acknowledge the strong pull exerted on us by the things and
people in our surroundings. "Lie down with dogs,
get up with fleas," some dog-hater once put it.

But whether, and for how long we lie down

with them, *is* at least somewhat up to us. And so is how we respond and react to the fleas. Not every participant agreed with the obviously wrong group decisions in Asch's conformity experiments. Not every German went along with Hitler; some were even executed for resisting the Nazis. And not everyone raised in crime and poverty succumbs to it. Otherwise Louis and others from such circumstances would never escape it as they certainly have. The pull of the things and people around us is strong, yes, but not irresistible.

This is not to deny the difficulty of circumstances you've been through or are facing right now. As we've seen, situations and the people around us can be very challenging and powerful. But odds are, if you've lived through difficulties, you can think right now of one way they helped make you a better person. Even in the case of abuse, a terrible thing. Most abusers were themselves abused as children, which shows the power of that very painful situation. But it is not all-powerful. The vast majority of abused people do not become abusers. Most do not let that situation define them; they go on to be good parents or spouses. In fact, such men and women often make a decided effort to be especially loving because of what was done to them. In Louis's case it's not a stretch to say that without his background his artistry would have turned out very differently. He played and sang from what he knew, and the world has never been the same.

The Armstrong biographies and Louis's own writings don't reveal him to have been extremely driven to escape poverty, as some people are. "I never did want to be a big mucky-muck star," he said. But escape poverty he did, to say the least. Until the day he left New Orleans to play in a riverboat orchestra, he was always working. Selling papers and working on a junk wagon as a child. Then working on coal carts, in coal yards, and on the docks unloading banana boats as a teen. And all the while practicing his cornet (a horn slightly rounder than a trumpet) and playing in bands whenever he could. So although it doesn't seem he was consciously striving to escape poverty, his attitude insured – as much as anything can – that he would not be a victim of it.

Poverty or any of a hundred other challenging conditions such as illness, difficult neighbors, or an abusive boss, are very serious, powerful things. I'm careful in choosing my words, though. I'm hesitant to label circumstances or events as "bad," because I've known people who became as positive or successful as they are *due to* the challenging events. Composer Wayne Shorter writes that "noble human behavior may remain dormant unless 'awakened' due to trials and tribulations." Perhaps something that seemed bad at one point in your life can even be seen as a blessing now when you look back on it.

A friend of mine had to have brain surgery. That's bad, right? Except it saved her life. That's good. The surgeon nicked a nerve that controls some facial muscles. Now my friend can't open her eye, although the eye itself still works. That's a bad thing, right? Can't you imagine someone being sad or bitter about that for the rest of her life? But a bit after the operation, she actually said she was glad it happened. You see, I misled you a bit; she can open the eye by hand. And she does so . . . when looking through a telescope. She's an amateur astronomer. A stargazer can see especially well with an eye that's been closed for days, making it very dilated and ready to take in a stunning amount of starlight.

Likewise, in a recent commercial, Michael J. Fox reports that Parkinson's has given him something to be thankful for: the ability to make a difference. Contemporary spiritual teachers Dr. Depak Chopra and Ekhart Tolle both routinely make the point that the externals of our world are really things that we interpret, and it is actually these perceptions that form the "world" each of us lives in mentally. Dr. Chopra writes, "Every situation is a choice in consciousness, and a recognition of that choice as the outer world." As bad as many of us would consider young Louis's circumstances, he did not see them that way. In fact he always spoke fondly of his childhood days and the characters he grew up around. "Every time I close my eyes blowing that trumpet of mine — I look right in the heart of good old New Orleans. . . . It has given me something to live for."

"But I'm not from poverty."

If you're not from poverty or such immediately challenging circumstances, you still might have an environment or background that can hold you back, even being from the middle class. In the documentary "Buena Vista Social Club," a film about the fantastic musical world of Cuba, there's a moment where an old Cuban says, "If we had followed the way of possessions, we would have disappeared long ago." He reminds me of the Buddha, who taught how craving leads to disappointment and suffering; and of Jesus, who said, "Your life does not consist of your possessions." Certainly Cuba has serious problems, but it also has far more dancing and live music than you find here in the United States. It's everywhere in Cuba. In fact, if you watch and listen to that film, it's hard to argue that Cuba doesn't have, well, more *soul* than America does. Gerry Goffin and Carol King wrote for the Monkees back in 1967 that creature comfort goals tend to numb our souls and make it hard for us to see.

No, I'm not advocating for the Amish life as I sit writing this book on a laptop (although some research does show the Amish being slightly happier than the general public). I'm merely trying to say that a relatively good life economically can have negative effects on someone just as rough circumstances can. We all know of wealthy children spoiled by their cushy circumstances just as a poor child can be stunted by poverty. Andrew Carnegie, a firsthand expert on wealth, actually said, "The richest heritage a man can have is to be born into poverty."

Yet many people from the upper class do go on to be of service to others. A good number of the Progressive Era's reformers were from wealthy families, as were the Roosevelts and Kennedys. Many have used their wealth to build businesses, fund community institutions, even eradicate diseases. These people's comfortable circumstances didn't define them and make them spoiled slugs, just as Louis's background didn't make him feel like a victim and stay stuck in poverty.

You're probably not one of the wealthy "One Percent," I know. But very possibly, you did have a relatively decent upbringing with abundant material goods, especially compared with much of the world. And decent circumstances when young might have led you to be living on achievement-drive or consumerism-autopilot now. Our culture certainly encourages it. How many commercial images are you bombarded with per day? Life is presented as being all about owning the new thing and looking right. Even our government of the people, by the people, and for the people refers to us as "consumers." But comfortable circumstances do not have to define us, numbing our souls, making us mindless consumer sheep. Even if you were a kid from a decent family (maybe even, like me, from the suburbs – a double whammy), you can still find some cause or higher purpose that gives your life meaning and helps other people too.

A contractor, rather than just earning his daily bread, can consciously give people the best roof or basement possible, to help them be warm and dry for a long time.

A businesswoman, rather than just enjoying the game and making some money, can be involved in a company that really benefits people and can focus on helping others.

A police officer, rather than just working a shift

and getting home, can be committed to justice and protecting people.

A teacher, rather than just doing a job to feed his kids and help them through college, can commit himself to a higher goal of helping young people become more intelligent and responsible.

A parent, rather than just surviving another day with only two more gray hairs, can consciously work at raising the best human beings possible. God knows we need as many compassionate, pro-active people as we can get.

I don't mean to assume you're *not* living for a higher goal. But I know how it goes: I am sometimes that teacher two paragraphs up. I know in my head that there are higher goals to pursue, but I'm often stuck for days on autopilot, performing a "day job." I merely offer the above contrasts as reminders, in case you too have been stuck on autopilot lately. We will have more to discuss about purpose near the end of the book. But for now, suffice it to say that the drudgery of daily life or the tyranny of the urgent do not have to dictate who we are or what we live for.

I am aware that saying middle class people can be handicapped in their own way might be insulting to those who come from poverty. Truly, I mean no offense; the point is just that each of us has circumstances that can limit us somehow. What is clear is that Louis did not let his circumstances limit who he was. He followed his inspiration to make music, worked very hard at it, and led a meaningful life. Instead of giving in to a very rough environment, he took what he saw and experienced, and played it back out to the world through his music.

True, you're not a great trumpet player born at the turn of the century. However, you *can* live like Louis: you can rise above your circumstances to daily create a life of purpose and fulfillment. May you meet with success and joy in that endeavor!

Practices

Some people believe there is a personal God or gods in control of things. Others believe in an intelligence or spirit pervading all things. If you hold to either of these paradigms, it can be helpful to give thanks to God or the universe for bringing you into tough circumstances or for bringing difficult people into your life. And even if you don't believe in any overarching power that might have brought you into tough times, you can still express gratitude for those circumstances.

Giving thanks for difficulties might sound odd. However, when we give thanks, we just plain feel better. It is an old cliché, but adopting an "attitude of gratitude" can work wonders in you and then through you.

Our logical, Western minds might still need a reason to give thanks for difficulties. Why give thanks for tough conditions? Try reflecting on what the circumstances taught you about yourself. Maybe you didn't handle them so well (I'm thinking of some specific times in *my* life right now, by the way). This can teach you where you might yet need to grow. Knowing yourself better is very valuable and worth giving thanks for.

Also, you can examine yourself and see how you *have* grown because of the difficulties. Louis certainly became the artist he was, partly due to his surroundings and experiences.

You might try copying and finishing these sentences in a notebook:

I am actually thankful for . . . [name a difficulty or challenge].

How I handled it teaches me about myself that I . . .

It helped me grow because . . .

We're a short-attention-span culture, trained to move quickly from one thing to the next. But if you will write the above sentences several times, over several days, they can be effective. They can help change your thoughts and feelings about the past, thus actually changing the interior world you live in. And as you grow in self-understanding, this in turn can help you be of more benefit to others. Like Louis, you can rise above difficult circumstances and even use them to bless other people.

Listening Suggestions

Links to audio and video files are found at
www.livelikelouis.com.

Despite his challenging environment during childhood and the racism of the Jim Crow South, Louis
made several records singing about a romanticized,
mythical Dixie. These include his theme song,
"When It's Sleepy Time Down South." The original
1931 version opens with some dialog between Louis
and his pianist who have met in the North and long
to go back home to eat some red beans and rice –
Louis's favorite food. This version has "darkies"
and "mammy" in it, but if you can accept these
words as being of their time, you'll hear Pops sing
in a very heartfelt manner. A later example of this
nostalgic style of song is "Do You Know What It
Means to Miss New Orleans?"

2 Keep the Rhythm Going

*in which Louis's mentors remind us
of the importance of encouragement*

"Louis Armstrong, how would you like to join our brass band?" This simple question was asked by the music instructor at a boys' reformatory in 1913. His eleven words changed the course not just of a life, but of American popular music. And it was all because a young instructor saw some good in a "bad" kid and decided to nurture his potential. That teacher, Peter Davis, along with Louis's later musical mentor, Joe Oliver, remind us of the importance of encouragement.

But how did Louis end up in New Orleans' Colored Waif's Home? If you recall, young Louis decided to fire off a gun on New Year's Eve, 1912. "Decided" is probably too strong a word to describe the actions of an eleven and a half year old boy, however. Knowing New Orleans' rowdy holiday traditions, Louis had swiped a pistol from one of his "stepfathers" and tucked it in his shirt. He and his quartet were out walking Rampart Street, singing for pennies when they heard someone across the street celebrating with a gun. His buddies yelled to Louis, "Go get him, Dipper!" So "Dippermouth" Armstrong obliged, impulsively firing his gun into the air. Writing about the incident decades later, Satchmo triumphantly recalled that his was the better, noisier gun and the other kid quickly took off.

Louis got away with firing his gun. Once. But the second time he fired shots into the air, it turned into a not-so-happy new year. His arms were immediately gripped tight from behind. A detective had been watching. Despite Louis's pleas to be sent home, the detective arrested the boy. Apparently the justice system moved a bit quicker back then: the very next day he was sentenced to the Colored Waif's Home, a military style reformatory five miles away from Louis's neighborhood. It might as well have been five hundred. The Home was surrounded by farms and gardens. Instead of hearing "King" Oliver's cornet belting out from a nearby honkeytonk, Louis now fell asleep to the sounds of nearby cattle and awoke with the chickens. It was one of the best things that ever happened to him.

Captain Jones, the superintendent, was strict but fair. The one hundred or so boys were awakened by bugle and practiced military drills in the yard. There was work to do every day, while the food and sleeping arrangements were spartan but adequate. The boys had to keep themselves and the Home clean. All learned trade skills. Some learned music.

Armstrong experts and Louis's own accounts differ as to when he first picked up a cornet (that slightly mellower version of the trumpet). He probably had a secondhand horn and was shown a few "licks" prior to his arrival at the Waif's Home. But without a doubt, the instruction he got at the Home from Mr. Davis was his first real musical training and his first experience in a band. But he almost didn't get that experience.

Mr. Davis didn't like him at first. Louis was a "bad" kid from a bad neighborhood. He hadn't just shoplifted or played truant, he had fired gunshots in public. But as the weeks went on, Mr. Davis softened. They say the child is father to the man, so it's easy to imagine Louis being very personable even at eleven. Mr. Davis would occasionally make eye contact with him and give a little smile. Since Louis had been abandoned by his own father, just a smile from the man made him "feel good inside." Occasionally Davis would speak to the boy. In 1954 Louis still vividly remembered how good even a little encouragement felt: "Gee, what a feeling, that coming from him!" Then after about six months, Davis approached Louis at supper and asked him that fateful question: Did he want to join the band? Louis was speechless. Mr. Davis had to repeat himself. Louis then happily accepted, washed up, and went to rehearsal. He was officially handed . . . a tambourine.

It wasn't exactly what he was hoping for. Cornet was the prestige instrument of the day, whether in a concert band like John Philip Sousa's or a little jazz combo back in the Third Ward of New Orleans. A gleaming, triumphant cornet, that's what Louis had been dreaming of playing. But it was not where a fellow began. Dues must be paid. So tambourine

came first. Louis made the most of it and his perseverance paid off. "Mr. Davis nodded with approval
which was all I needed. His approval was all important for any boy who wanted a musical career."
Davis promoted Louis to alto horn. Louis continued
to practice and earn Mr. Davis's approval.

Then a lucky break: the Home's bugler was released to his parents. Now was Louis's chance! Mr.
Davis asked Louis to be the bugler. He polished the
horn, practiced hard, and played well. His dili-
gence and talent earned him the right to play cornet. Mr. Davis taught him "Home, Sweet Home,"
and Louis later recalled, "I was in seventh heaven.
Unless I was dreaming, my ambition had been realized." I smile every time I read that remembrance,
hearing in it a boy's happiness and pride.

After practicing diligently on cornet, Louis was
approached by Mr. Davis: "Louis, I am going to
make you leader of the band." The boy leapt up
and whooped for joy right in front of his mentor.
He would lead the band in its resplendent uniforms
all throughout greater New Orleans. They played in
the frequent parades for which the Crescent City is
still famous, and at many picnics and social events.
The boy was now a musician and a leader. The
Louis Armstrong we know and love was on his
way, thanks to the perception and encouragement
of Mr. Peter Davis.

A King, but Not Too Proud to Be a Mentor

I mentioned "King" Oliver in passing, a few para-

graphs back. By Louis's teen years, Joe Oliver was
the top cornet player in the parade bands and jazz
combos of New Orleans. As such, he took his place
in a lineage of local cornet kings. Rival Bunk Johnson was giving Oliver a run for his money as top
player, but Louis considered Joe Oliver the best.
Louis wrote,

> The way I see it, the greatest musical crea-
> tions came from his horn – and I've heard a
> lot of them play. . . . Joe Oliver *created*
> things. . . . When he played his cornet there
> were always happiness.

As local cornet master and star of the Onward
Brass Band, Joe Oliver might simply have enjoyed
his fame and moved onward and upward in the
musical world. Instead he chose also to teach and
encourage a young hanger-on who would eventually surpass his master. In 1960 Louis would write
that Oliver "had a heart as big as a whale when it
came to helping the underdog in music such as me.
I was just a kid, Joe saw I had possibilities and he'd
go out of his way to help me or any other ambitious
kid who were interested in their instrument as I
were."

When Joe was done with a parade, he'd let the
teenage Louis carry his horn. Oliver later gave him
an old cornet which Louis "guarded with his life."
King Oliver was willing to show him "anything I
wanted to know" on the horn. Moreover, Mrs.
Oliver would have Louis run errands for her, often
invited him to stay for supper, and in many ways

treated him like a son. This adopted family made quite an impression, as Louis would later make clear in an unpublished memoir. "I shall never forget how Joe Oliver and his wife, Mrs. Stella Oliver, were so nice to me in New Orleans, when I was quite a youngster."

One story marvelously illustrates the interest Joe Oliver took in the young Louis Armstrong. Around 1917, Armstrong and a buddy put together their own combo. Bands would advertise upcoming appearances by playing while riding through the streets on a wagon. When competing bands would meet, they would have an impromptu "cutting" contest to determine who was better and drum up business. Oliver gave Louis a special signal: if their bands were to meet, Louis should stand up so Oliver would see him. Oliver's band would then play a couple of numbers to show who was boss, but not embarrass the youngsters too badly. Oliver's group would also pointedly omit a tune usually played as a comical dismissal of a vanquished band.

One time the wagons met and Louis forgot to stand up. Without that signal Oliver's band competed full force and demolished the boys. Oliver later gave Louis an earful for not signaling him to go easy on his young friend. Mentor and apprentice swiftly patched it up, however, over a bottle of beer. This was especially impressive to Louis since King Oliver was a bit tight with his money, at least in the drink-buying department. "But for me he would do anything," he wrote.

Oliver left New Orleans in 1918, part of the

Great Migration of Southern blacks to find freedom from Jim Crow and poverty. First he toured. Then he established King Oliver's Creole Jazz Band in 1922 and became ensconced at Chicago's famed Lincoln Gardens ballroom. He was the talk of that toddlin' town. And who took Oliver's place back in New Orleans? Louis Armstrong, of course. From his work in dance bands and his prominent role in the Tuxedo Brass Band, Louis's reputation grew and spread. "I could go into any part of New Orleans without being bothered. Everybody loved me and just wanted to hear me." With Louis obviously possessing serious talent, it might seem inevitable to us modern, mobile people that he too would leave New Orleans. But Louis was really a homebody. He loved his mother's red beans and rice, and he had seen too many friends leave home and meet with trouble. "I had made up my mind that I would not leave New Orleans unless the King sent for me."

The king beckoned.

Oliver's telegrams gave a young, home-loving, Southern black man the courage to board the Illinois Central line and leave everything he knew behind him, armed only with a valise, a cornet, and a fish sandwich lovingly packed by his mother. When he got off the train in Chicago, Stella and Joe Oliver fed him and made rooming arrangements. Louis played second cornet that night with his idol and father figure. At the end of the evening, Oliver even let the young man take a solo. They soon became famous for playing "breaks" in the music together in harmony. Usually in such breaks all the other musicians suddenly stop and let one soloist shine for a couple of measures. But Oliver shared the spotlight with Louis, the two of them displaying a musical affinity that became legendary.

A decision to tour broke up that great band. Louis and his wife, Lil, the group's piano player, were the only two who stayed with Oliver. After the tour, Oliver's Creole Jazz Band was no more. The King took a position in another group, and Louis got the call to go to New York, to the top black dance orchestra there. Oliver and Armstrong went their separate ways, professionally. But for the rest of his life, Louis would talk of how he felt about "Papa" Joe, who had taken the time to teach and encourage him: "I can never stop loving Joe Oliver. He was always ready to come to my rescue when I needed someone to tell me about life and its little intricate things, and help me out of difficult situations."

The Power of Encouragement

I freely acknowledge that I am not to teaching, parenting, or living, what Joe Oliver was to cornet playing. Nevertheless, there are plenty of people I come across in my life I can encourage in some way. The German poet Goethe wrote, "Correction does much, but encouragement does more." And education expert Linda Albert advises my fellow teachers and me, "Encouragement is the most powerful tool we possess." They couldn't be righter. Think back to people who encouraged you. I'll bet you remember their attitude. It was positive. They had confidence in you and it showed. The root of "courage," by the way, is the Latin word *cor*, or "heart." So the people who encouraged you spoke to your heart and gave you strength to face a challenge and believe in yourself.

Sometimes it seems we're drowning in words lately, especially if you browse through cable TV or talk radio. Encouragement, however, is one area where words *are* often necessary and can actually do some lasting good. Go to any youth sporting event and you'll hear how natural it is for parents to yell encouraging words to their children. Out on the soccer fields in my town, you're liable to hear parents yell things like "Stay with him, Brett," or "Good save, Liz." There's no instruction there, just words meant to fire the kid up a bit and help her performance. But does it really do any good?

A team of sports science researchers in Pennsylvania set out in 2002 to investigate that very question. They pre-tested a number of men and women on treadmill performance; then divided them into groups receiving either frequent, infrequent, or no words of encouragement during a second attempt. Comparing their pre- and post-tests, those who were encouraged more frequently (every 20 or 60 seconds) put forth "significantly greater maximum effort," felt less tired, and even had better oxygen usage. Just hearing words of encouragement does change how we feel and act.

That's scientific evidence from the laboratory. Here are some examples of words of encouragement recently overheard in real life:

Someone is having a hard time finding a job. Her friend commiserates but also adds, "Hang in there, the right job is out there somewhere."

A child is having a hard time with the challenge of helping clean a relative's vacant house. His dad says, "I have confidence in you," and compliments the boy's perseverance when he finishes the task.

A colleague is thinking about making a career change. His friend offers advice and adds, "But I know you'll be good at whichever one you pick."

A student is having a hard time choosing a topic for a demonstration speech. The teacher doesn't try to solve the problem for her; instead she asks several questions to guide her, then says, "I'm sure you'll choose a good topic." (She eventually picked a great topic, by the way: a magic trick that still stumps those of us who missed her speech!)

A lot in our culture seems set up to promote and benefit from strife and nastiness. Sharing encouragement is one easy way to counter that trend and give the universe a gentle nudge back in the direction of kindness and cooperation. As bandleader Stan Kenton put it, "When you get to the top, don't forget to send the elevator down for the next guy." Hearing about the encouragers in Louis's life and remembering those recent examples from my own experience motivate me to want to do likewise. Maybe it will be just through a few words of hope to someone at home or at work; maybe through a more purposeful mentoring relationship. Whatever your situation, you too can be like Peter Davis and King Oliver. You can encourage a friend or co-worker to grow or take a chance or keep on going during a tough time. You probably won't make someone the next cornet king. But you *will* make a difference.

Practices

Every morning for a week, before you start your day, try thinking of someone who has encouraged you. Recollect what words he or she said to cheer or hearten you, and how the words were delivered. Bring to mind how the encourager's attitude empowered you and made you feel. Then write the person's name on a piece of paper and put it in your pocket; or on a sticky note placed where you'll see it during your day. Each time you notice it, say to yourself,

"Be like _____ today."

To take it a step further, bring to mind the people you generally interact with and see if anyone seems particularly in need of encouragement. Resolve to find a way to cheer or strengthen that person today. Plan the words in advance, or leave it to the moment, but seek him or her out and be an encourager. Remember the effect that Peter Davis and Joe Oliver had on Louis. When you change how one person feels or acts, you have changed the world.

Listening Suggestions

Links to audio and video files are found at
www.livelikelouis.com.

"Snake Rag," by King Oliver's Creole Jazz Band in 1923, is a fun, comical piece. You can hear Louis and King Oliver taking their famous breaks together when everything in the music stops but them. You also get a good example of polyphonic music, the essence of early jazz. Literally it means "many sounds," which refers to the wind instruments all playing seemingly independent lines at the same time, yet meshing together gloriously.

"Chimes Blues," recorded the day before, is the King Oliver piece Ken Burns selected for his terrific CD anthology of Louis's music. Again, there is wonderful polyphonic playing, plus you can hear the future Mrs. Armstrong simulating chimes. You'll hear an extended solo about two minutes into the record: it's Satchmo's first recorded solo. Writer and Armstrong scholar Gary Giddins says when you hear it you're hearing the future.

Finally, on this book's companion website you'll find links to two segments from the old TV show *I've Got a Secret*. I heartily recommend viewing them. I won't reveal the secret, but the ending is one of the most touching things I've ever seen.

3   I Get Ideas

*in which Louis reminds us
of the value of an open mind*

Over the years, a number of keen-eyed observers
have noticed that in some photographs you can
spot Pops wearing a small medallion. This particular piece of jewelry has piqued people's curiosity
enough that there's even a question and answer
thread about it on the *Yahoo!Answers* website. The
interest is because the medallion Louis wore relig-
iously in his later years was a Star of David. Why
would Louis Armstrong, a black man baptized
Catholic in New Orleans, wear the symbol of Juda-
ism? The answer lies in a family's kindness to him,
and in Louis's openness to a wide variety of ideas.

One of the most important factors in Louis's ris-
ing above poverty and a crime-saturated neighborhood was how people nurtured and looked out for
him. We've already met his mother, Peter Davis,
and the Olivers. In addition to them, Louis was
sheltered and looked-after by the Karnofskys, a
Jewish family he worked for as a boy. They were a
family of peddlers who had come from Lithuania,

and their generous treatment of one child would pay huge dividends for American music. Little Louis assisted in buying up rags, bones, and other junk. He also rode along on their wagon to help the Karnofskys sell coal to prostitutes in New Orleans' Storyville red-light district. To advertise their business in the age before television commercials and internet pop-up ads, the two Karnofsky brothers employed Louis to blow on a tin horn to announce their wagon's approach. One day the wagon passed a pawn shop; from behind the window, an old cornet grabbed Louis's attention. It was priced at five dollars, though, far more than the boy had. To help Louis buy the instrument, Morris Karnofsky advanced him two dollars. Louis paid the rest in fifty-cent installments out of his pay.

Perhaps as important as lending Louis the money for a horn, the Karnofskys were also very encouraging. "The Karnofsky family kept reminding me that I had talent," Louis wrote.

> Although I could not play a good tune Morris applauded me just the same, which made me feel very good. As a young boy coming up, the people whom I worked for were very much concerned about my future in music. They could see that I had music in my soul. They really wanted me to be something in life. And music was it. Appreciating my every effort.

In this recollection written in his late sixties, you can't miss hearing the fondness Louis Armstrong still felt for that family. The Karnofskys were whites who dared treat a black child like one of the family. After a day of junk peddling and an evening of selling coal, they would feed him, leading to his lifelong affinity for matzos. Before sending Louis home for the night, the Karnofskys would let him participate in a family ritual as they sang the baby to sleep. "They were always warm and kind to me, which was very noticeable to me – just a kid who could use a little word of kindness, something that a kid could use at seven, and just starting out in the world." Their kind treatment greatly affected Louis: "I will love the Jewish people all of my life," he wrote near the end of it.

As to the Star of David necklace itself, it was given to Louis by his longtime manager, Joe Glaser, who was Jewish. The mid-1930s was a low period in Pops' career. Glaser helped Louis sort out his business affairs, resolving a potentially lethal conflict between two mob-connected agents both claiming Satchmo as their own. Also, the contract he secured for Louis with Decca Records greatly expanded Satchmo's popularity. For more than thirty years, Glaser would oversee Louis's career, helping him reach countless people and become an American icon. Louis had planned to publish his memories of the Karnofskys and he dedicated the work to Glaser, "The best Friend / That I've ever had / May the Lord Bless Him / Watch over him always." Because of the Karnofskys' care and Glaser's attentive management, Louis Armstrong, a black son of the South, felt warmly toward the Jewish people all his life.

Cats of Any Color

Louis was also open-minded about race. "He was the least prejudiced musician I ever knew," recalled photographer George Schnitzer. This is not to say he was ignorant of his country's racial problems. That was impossible. In fact, one of his most famous quips came after a friend asked him what was new. Louis's reply: "Nothin' new. White folks still ahead." And we'll read in chapter eight how Louis jeopardized his career with some deliberately blunt comments about discrimination in the 1950s. But although he was very aware of racism, he was open-minded when it came to people and their race. "White audiences from all over the world picked up on my music, from the first note that I ever blown. And until these days they are still with me," he wrote in 1969. He spoke glowingly of the other great jazz trumpeter of the Roaring Twenties, the German-descended Bix Beiderbecke: "Those pretty notes went right through me."

Moreover, Louis made one of the first jazz records with a racially mixed group. On that record date, Pops was very moved by the playing of white trombonist (and future close friend) Jack Teagarden. Louis ascended a stepladder and sat up near a skylight to absorb Teagarden's beautiful sounds as he warmed up. The recording engineer had to invite Louis back down to make the record. Describing the white trombonist's musicality, Louis placed his hand over his heart, saying, "It moves me, it moves me right through here."

In 1947, as the swing band era was ending,

Louis put together a great small group he called the All Stars. Though the personnel would change over the next two decades, this would be the group he played and toured with relentlessly for the rest of his days. Right from the start it was racially mixed; and there at the beginning was a white man who was about as close to a peer as Louis had: trombone virtuoso Jack Teagarden, whom Louis had ascended the stepladder to hear in 1929. Louis declared, "Those people who make the restrictions, they don't know nothing about music, it's no crime for cats of any color to get together and blow."

On tour in the Middle East in 1959, Pops played in both Lebanon and Israel. In each country he was challenged by reporters, for making music for the Other. "Let me tell you something, man. That horn, you see that horn? That horn ain't prejudiced. A note's a note in any language."

Eclectic Musical Tastes

In the late 1930s, jazz aficionados were critical of Louis for abandoning the "pure" jazz of his records of the 1920s. He was now recording pop tunes with a larger band backing his playing and singing. But the critics were ignoring the full output of his earlier recordings, many of which featured singing, talking, even comedy. Louis never considered himself purely a jazz player; he was an overall musician and entertainer. First on the riverboats, then in Chicago, Louis played in orchestras that performed all kinds of music, from waltzes to polkas to light clas-

sics to "hot" jazz. This served to broaden his already wide-ranging taste in music. Louis's early
record collection included opera star Enrico Caruso
and Irish tenor John McCormack. Biographer Terry
Teachout believes their expressive style helped influence Pops' soaring, expansive trumpet solos.

Louis's broad taste in music was reflected in
various ways. He recorded with country music pioneer Jimmie Rodgers in 1930 and with Johnny Cash
in 1970. Late in life he made a whole album of country songs and one entirely of Disney tunes. He died
with over 600 reels of tape onto which he had transferred much of his 1200-item record collection of
classics, opera, pop, Broadway, and modern jazz. In
1968 Louis listed Barbara Streisand's "People" as a
record he'd take to a desert island. He praised the
Beatles, describing them as "right outa the old spiri-
tuals and soul and country music and jazz." His favorite music other than his own was the Guy
Lombardo band. Though most jazz fans found
Lombardo's Royal Canadians "syrupy" or "corny,"
Louis liked their danceable beat and the fact that
they never strayed far from a song's melody. Judg-
ing one of Lombardo's tunes once, Pops exclaimed,
"Give this son of a gun *eight* stars! Lombardo!"
Satchmo's taste in music was nothing if not wide-
ranging.

The Value of Openness

Being open to many different styles of music is an
example of a cluster of similar personality traits dis-

covered by researchers. Using math to analyze thousands of personality tests given in the 20th century, psychologists found that many specific personality traits are linked together. For instance, individuals who are very "orderly" also tend to be very "precise" and "punctual." And people low in one tend to be low in the other two. Such similarities have led behavioral scientists to recognize five major clusters of personality traits they call the Big Five. One such mega-trait is Openness to Experience. And if anyone ever would have scored high in Openness, it was Louis Armstrong.

"Openness to Experience" sounds at first hearing as if it should be about bungee jumping or scuba diving, and indeed it could include these. But psychologists view Openness as being more about interests in diverse areas, being imaginative, and being intellectually and artistically curious. Of course, some people aren't like that at all, and that's no sin or crime. Rating low in this trait doesn't make someone a bad person. Like many traits, we need people at both ends of the spectrum, and when it comes to Openness, we need some meat-n-potatoes, normalcy-is-good folks, for sure. Just as we need the folks at the other end, like Louis. Once, when learning about the jazz age in U.S. History class, I and my students looked at some pretty far-out paintings by artists of the Harlem Renaissance. Some students responded by proclaiming the works weird, while others thought them interesting or cool. (And of course, there were plenty of kids in the middle.)

Research with identical twins reared apart has

shown that about fifty percent of the differences among us in any given trait is due to our genes. Someone born to real meat-n-potatoes parents will probably never become a wide-open urban hipster, and that's fine. But fifty percent from DNA still leaves about half our personality resulting from our upbringing and environment. So we're not fated through our genes to turn out exactly a certain way in any trait. Rather, it seems we're born with a set "range." Where we end up within that range is affected by our environment. And that environment includes much over which we have control.

Through what we read, view, and listen to, and by the people we hang out with, we can end up reinforcing our own likes and preferences. This is natural, but treading the same path over and over can turn it into a rut. On the other hand, we can stretch and experience things outside our proverbial comfort zones. Being open to new ideas might even help you live a longer, more productive life. Scientists have known for a while that simply keeping the brain active, even just by doing crosswords, can delay the onset of Alzheimer's disease. Now, recent research shows that learning a new language is especially helpful in delaying the course of that disorder. Of course aside from biological benefits, searching out new ideas or perspectives can help you grow in other ways.

Here I should mention the book you now hold (or read on your tablet device) came about from a little out-of-the-comfort-zone serendipity. While walking past the "new books" section at my local Mind and Soul Center (the public library), I spied a paperback titled *Me 2.0* in the business section, not one of my usual haunts. But after looking it over, I was intrigued, took it home (after checking it out, of course) and entered the world of "personal branding" under the guidance of author and consultant Dan Schawbel. In his book, he recommends "writing your book" as if doing so is a matter of course, something anyone can and should do. So, thanks to a book I wouldn't ordinarily find myself reading, inspiration struck, hard-but-enjoyable work began, and this book was created. It makes you wonder what other adventures might be in store, through future wandering away from the comfortable.

Recommending an excursion away from the familiar is not to say you shouldn't deeply hold some beliefs or outlooks, or enjoy one type of art or magazine or even person over another. To paraphrase a country song, you have to stand for something or you'll fall for anything. But we can hold our beliefs and enjoy what we enjoy without insulting or belittling others of a different opinion, as some people feel the need to do. And, by considering other positions or approaches, we'll remember that the people who hold differing viewpoints are just as smart and worthwhile as we are, no matter how loudly some pundit might tell us otherwise.

Louis Armstrong's love of the Jewish people, his acceptance of whites in an overtly racist age, and his broad taste in music remind us of the value of openness. Even if you were born to be essentially a meat-n-potatoes person, you might try a different cut of meat or swap in a new side dish every now and then. Prepare to be pleasantly surprised!

Practices

Option A, food:

Let's begin with the meat-n-potatoes metaphor and take it literally. Buy at the store, or sample at a restaurant, a food you've never had before. Even if you end up not caring for it, try to imagine why some people find it enjoyable. And if you do like it, give thanks for a new pleasure in life.

Option B, politics:

Read an article by a reasonable spokesperson of a viewpoint different from yours. Stay far away from extreme blowhards of any political persuasion unless you need a laugh. If you're more liberal, try reading David Frum; if you're more conservative, Robert Reich. Listen for the underlying assumptions that are different from yours, and why they might make sense to other people. One website that has reasonable arguments from both sides is *The Moderate Voice* at www.themoderatevoice.com.

Option C, music:

Deliberately listen to some music you ordinarily wouldn't. A student just had me listen to some Justin Bieber a couple of days ago, and you know what? It wasn't bad. It was fun and listenable, certainly no worse than a lot of other things I've heard.

Currently the iTunes store has a free single of the week and a "discovery download" featuring a different genre each week. Try to hear the good in what you choose, and consider why it appeals to its fans. Dancing, as always, remains an option.

Listening Suggestions

Links to audio and video files are found at
www.livelikelouis.com.

The fun "Knockin' a Jug" is the record made in 1929 after Louis came down off his stepladder to play with trombone genius Jack Teagarden. Teagarden is the first soloist, and you can hear why Louis was so knocked out.

In 1930 Louis performed on "Blue Yodel #9" by the early country artist Jimmie Rodgers. You can fast forward forty years and experience the same piece in a televised duet with Johnny Cash.

We'll have much more to say about the haunting "Black and Blue" in chapter eight. But for now, see if you can notice a little Eastern European influence Satchmo occasionally flavors this record with. Some writers believe this musical flavoring originated in his time with the Lithuanian Karnofskys. After all, sixty years later Louis wrote, "It was the Jewish family who instilled in me singing from the heart."

Another song in a minor key with a bit of Karnofsky flavoring is "Chim Chim Cheree." Pops almost always stuck to tunes in a major (happy) key, so his extended take on this Disney tune is fairly rare. Plus there's the unmistakable joy he has in singing "a-chimmie-chimmie-chimmie."

4   Now You Has Jazz

in which Louis shows us we can
go with the flow when the unexpected occurs

It doesn't get any more ciché than this: "When life hands you a lemon . . ." You know the rest. Never mind that some of us *like* lemons, it's often hard to see an unexpected change as an opportunity. But making lemonade is just what Satchmo did many times in his storied career.

For one example, let's travel back to 1926 Chicago, the heart of the Roaring Twenties. Louis had been a sensation there, gone and made his mark in New York, then returned to become an even bigger star in the capital of the Midwest. He put together a group of the best New Orleans musicians he could gather, to create a series of records now acclaimed as some of the greatest ever made. It was in making these records that Louis really started to soar and established jazz as a soloist's art. (Also, it's from these small group sessions that NASA chose the recording now zipping out of our solar system on the Voyager spacecraft.)

Picture Louis in an early recording studio with a

trombonist, clarinetist, pianist, and banjo player arranged around a big horn like that of a Victrola (the
old, acoustic type of record player). Their sound
waves would be funneled to a stylus cutting a long,
spiral groove into a rotating wax master disc. After
making a mold from this master, many copies of a
record could be pressed. Louis and the group were
recording a song called "Heebie Jeebies," a slang
term for feeling anxious or excited. While playing
the happy-sounding, medium tempo piece, the unexpected occurred. To stop the "take" and start the
whole thing over would waste a master disc. Let's
let Louis himself tell how he salvaged the situation:

> I dropped the paper with the lyrics – right in
> the middle of the tune . . . And I did not
> want to stop and spoil the record which was
> moving along so wonderfully . . . So when I
> dropped the paper, I immediately turned
> back into the horn and started to Scatting . . .
> Just as nothing had happened . . . When I
> finished the record I just knew the recording
> people would throw it out . . . And to my
> surprise they all came running out of the
> controlling booth and said – "Leave That
> In."

This is the creation myth of scat singing, an
element of jazz in which, you might recall, a singer
improvises with meaningless syllables in place of
words. (Feel free to leave for a minute and listen to
"Heebie Jeebies" on the companion website.) This
wasn't the first scat singing on record as many be-

lieve, much less the first scat singing ever. But Louis's spirit and inventiveness sure put it on the map, selling an unheard-of 40,000 copies. In fact, it's called "scat" singing because that's a particular syllable Pops used on the record. When Louis starts scatting, there are no words getting in the way, for our conscious minds to interpret. We're about as directly in touch with another's joy as we can be, like hearing my kids yell, "Woo hoo!" when finding out they're going to the beach. But with Louis the joy is improvised artistically, with a banjo in the background. It doesn't get much better than that.

Hello, Hit Record

For a second example of adapting to the unexpected, we'll jump ahead forty years or so. But we'll bring that banjo with us, since it plays a role in another key recording in Louis's life. By late 1963 Louis's group, the All Stars, had toured all over the world and were in great demand around the country and on TV. Still, Louis and his manager craved another hit record that would get significant radio play, as had happened with "Blueberry Hill" in the late 1940s and "Mack the Knife" in the '50s. He hadn't recorded anything for a couple of years, and the producer decided to have him record a couple of contemporary show tunes. The first seemed tailor-made for the pop charts. "A Lot of Livin' to Do" was from the popular show and movie *Bye Bye Birdie*. It had a fun beat and lyrics about going out and living large. A no-brainer for Satchmo, in other words. The only other tune scheduled for the session was from an obscure (as in "hadn't-even-opened-yet") musical by a little-known composer, Jerry Herman. Louis and the boys would record the title song.

Pops didn't much care for it. It seemed too plain. He even changed a few lyrics, throwing in his own name. Nevertheless the record seemed bland. The call went out for a banjoist to add a little flavor. He soon arrived and added an intro, and the record was made. Pops promptly forgot about both tunes, and Kapp Records released the single with "Livin'" as the A-side. On the B-side was that song Louis thought too simple: "Hello, Dolly."

The Broadway show opened in early 1964 and became a huge hit in New York. That, plus the excellence of Louis's record, led to his getting some serious airplay on the radio. But the All Stars were out on tour in the Midwest, literally out of the loop. Pretty soon they were getting requests from their audiences for "Hello Dolly." It was such an obscure thing when they had recorded it, Louis couldn't even remember what it was. Arvell Shaw, his bassist, reminded him and they looked around for the lead sheets (sketched-out written parts) from the recording session. Lost. They telegrammed their office in New York: What to do? The answer: go buy a copy of their own recording so they could learn their own tune. But the record was selling like proverbial hotcakes; they looked and looked, but there was none to be found. The office had to fly Louis a recording. The band listened to it several times, relearned their parts and played it that night.

Finally the crowd got what it wanted. Louis got eight curtain calls.

Perhaps you remember Paul Harvey, whose radio broadcast always told a story with one important detail left out. When he revealed it, he would intone in his inimitable way, "And now you know the *rest* . . . of the story." This story likewise has one last little twist like that. The record of "Hello, Dolly" grew and grew in popularity until it became one of those records where you couldn't avoid it if you tried. It rose on the charts until it reached number one in May 1964, the last number one recording by a jazz artist (who was also the oldest person ever to reach that top spot). Biographer Terry Teachout believes it was the amazing success of this record that propelled Louis from jazz star to cultural icon. Since "Hello Dolly" became the number one record, that means Louis must have knocked a previous act out of first place. Who was that group he toppled from first place, which they had held for fourteen weeks? A relatively new act from overseas, a little group with funny haircuts and an oddly-spelled name: the Beatles.

Another, Cheesy Food Metaphor

In both stories, Louis adjusts to the unexpected. The first curveball is pretty small, a dropped piece of paper. But he hits a home run. Another artist might have said, "Hold it. Cut. Set up a new master and let's take it from the top." But Louis starts scatting. The second unexpected event is a bit more challenging: audiences demanding an unknown tune, and the musicians having to scurry to find and relearn it. But relearn it they do, bringing joy to thousands of hearers.

Aside from these two anecdotes, in his career Louis had to make other, more substantial adjustments to change. In the mid-1930s, a decade and a half of playing the trumpet hard every night caught up with Pops and he suffered lip injuries. Though he kept his high notes, he was never quite as nimble as in the twenties. So he and his record label had him focus more on pop songs and singing (though of course he kept on trumpeting, too). After World War II, tastes and economics changed. Big swing bands were no longer viable. Many were folding. Few big band leaders would retain their place in the public eye after the war. But Louis did. He changed with the times. Though he hated to lay off a dozen or more men, he formed a small group and became the highest-paid act in jazz.

But he didn't retreat back to early New Orleans-style music, even though his group looked like that type of combo. And though he didn't embrace the new, intellectual be-bop style of the late 1940s and '50s (he *had* been playing since 1913, after all) his style and repertoire did change with the times. Once when listening to an old recording of a good early jazz group, Louis and his musicians broke up in laughter at how dated and corny it sounded. Some people criticized his All Star concerts for being predictable. True, the group always opened the same way (not an unusual practice), and the hits Louis *had* to play did add up over the years. But perusing his programs over two decades of shows, critics find great variety, with the group continually dropping and adding songs, including many then-current pop tunes. Louis Armstrong the self-avowed Beatles fan even recorded John Lennon's "Give Peace a Chance" in 1970! Louis could have stagnated or gone backwards after the big band era collapsed. But his resilience resulted in his becoming even more popular as he aged, like a fine wine.

Or a fine cheese, our second food metaphor in this chapter on adjusting to change. One common phrase for new circumstances being imposed on you is "having your cheese moved." This metaphor entered pop culture in the late 1990s thanks to Spencer Johnson's bestselling book, *Who Moved My Cheese?* It's a little tale of two mice and two people who live in a maze and get used to where the cheese always is. One day it's gone. How will they handle it? Spoiler alert: the moral of this a-mazing tale is, "Change happens, go with the flow." But that's easier said than done, which is probably the reason for the book's millions of readers. Though we like variety in little things, we generally prefer consistency in how the world works. This probably harkens back to thousands of years of living in the wild, where the unexpected could be not only bad but possibly life-threatening.

Moreover, the unexpected is especially troubling when it is imposed from the outside. Notice the title is not, "Hey, my cheese moved." No, *someone* has moved it, forcing you to adjust, reminding you you're not in control. If you want to annoy someone fast, tell them they have to learn a new way to do something they've been doing for a while. Even young people. I got quite a chuckle when Facebook changed its format and I overheard my high school students complaining about it. "Why do they always have to change everything?!" Just wait, kids. Just wait.

Change and the unexpected often mean work: time and energy spent on something we'd rather not be doing, like learning a new system at the office, how to program a new phone, even how to place your garbage when the city gets new trucks. In my field, it's online teaching, a pretty big move of the cheese, a game changer, really. Even when our rational minds can see there will be a benefit to the change (as there certainly is to online learning), there's an annoyance that accompanies having to do things differently. In fact, perceiving the need to adjust to something is one of the key components of stress, especially when you're in doubt about your ability to meet the challenge successfully. Even positive changes we choose to make can be stressful. Try getting married or having a child.

But as Dr. Johnson points out in his fable, change is a fact of life. Shift happens. And the rate of change, the speed at which things are shifting is itself speeding up. Even *change* is changing! For several hundred thousand years as *Homo sapiens*, change was rarer and slower. You lived as your ancestors had, with pretty much the same beliefs, customs, and technology. Now, even a decade ago can seem almost like another world. Compare the Archie-n-Jughead malt shop culture of 1960 to post-Woodstock 1970. And for our long-ago ancestors, when change did happen, it was often predictable and orderly, like the procession of the seasons or migration of prey. Ironically, people could order their lives around change. Now in many areas, especially technology, the rate of change is exponential and unpredictable, at least to most laypeople. Living happily in 1994, I had no idea that in 2000 I'd be buying Christmas presents and getting my news via some newfangled "interweb" gizmo. So, unlike our ancestors who dealt with predictable, cyclic changes, we really don't know what accelerating alterations will bring. The cheese is being moved faster and faster, and it's mutating into new kinds we've never tasted before.

This is not what we're designed or evolved for. But it's how things are. We can curse the dark or light a candle; complain about the moving cheese, or lace up our sneakers and run with it. Louis was obviously a sneaker-lacer. Since faster, unexpected change is now the status quo and since it is by nature stressful, how can we be more like Louis and go with the flow?

How to Be More Resilient

The American Psychological Association has produced a helpful online resource with some good suggestions on how to be better at rolling with the flow. One is to accept that the unexpected is very much part of life. Permanency is an illusion and a craving (more on this in Practices at the end of this chapter). The sooner we acknowledge that change and the unexpected are everywhere, the better we can adapt. It's also helpful if you're stressing about the change to acknowledge and say to yourself, "I'm worrying and stressing about this change. It's a very natural reaction." You are by no means a bad or odd person for resisting change or disliking the unexpected, especially if it does come with very challenging consequences. But it will help if you consciously acknowledge the change and your response as being what they are.

You can also purposefully keep things in perspective. You can think of people who are facing worse. And you can consciously try to see the potential positives. This gets back to the "make lemonade" idea. In my profession's paradigm shift to online teaching, though it could result in jobs lost, there will be other positions created. And though I might miss the fun my students and I have in class, I might also welcome not having to be the behavior manager of thirty teenagers forced to be in the same room for an hour.

Aside from this cognitive (thought) work of accepting the unexpected and looking for positives, another suggestion is to take some concrete action. Even if you never come to *embrace* unexpected change (again, a quite natural response), you can still do something. When the cheese moves, your chance of starving goes up dramatically if you do nothing. Taking even a small step toward the new cheese will increase your chance of future success, plus you'll feel much better than worrying or doing nothing. I can worry about the trend towards online teaching or I can take a summer course on how to do it. Even though I'd rather be kayaking (or writing about Louis), just that small bit of progress will reduce my worrying and make me more likely to succeed as the changes happen. And rolling with one change will make me more resilient in future disruptions.

Look around your world: family, work, religion, public affairs, even sports. What are changes you can see coming either now or in the future? You can acknowledge that change is unavoidable and that these specific changes are happening. And you can do something, even something small to adjust to them. You have adjusted to change in the past and you can again in the future. Who knows? Maybe your new cheese will eventually make you burst into some joyful scat singing!

Practices

One way to cling less to the status quo is first to recognize the attachment; then consciously remember the impermanence of all things. Think of any aspect of your life and you can probably remember pretty quickly how it used to be different. And the permanence of you? Forget about it. You're constantly dying and being reborn at the cellular level. Even your nerve cells, which don't die and reproduce, still over time exchange the matter that makes them up. That exchange is what makes "life" life after all. So even once you reach adulthood, there will still be several more "yous," considering just the physical body and its matter. And that's totally aside from how we change mentally and emotionally over the years.

Even the most solid, nonliving physical object is really an event. Remember your chemistry. Any seemingly-solid stone you hold in your hand is mostly empty space down at the atomic level. And its tiny little atoms are all in motion. All is in motion. All is change.

Here is an easy guided relaxation practice, to help remember our true state of impermanence and to be more resilient.

Sit comfortably in a quiet room. Notice your breathing. Let your mind be as relaxed as you can.

Wait about three breaths. After that, use this pair of sentences from a renowned teacher of spirituality, Thich Nhat Hanh:

Each time you inhale, think,
  "Breathing in, I calm my body."

As you exhale, think,
  "Breathing out, I smile."

Don't force a smile, but don't try to stifle it if one arises. Take the eminent philosopher Paul McCartney's advice and let it be. Breathe at whatever tempo feels natural; your body will do what's right for you. You can even use shorthand after a few breaths, simply thinking "calm" on the in-breath, "smile" on the out.

After several repetitions of that pair of thoughts, try moving through the following sequence about impermanence. Do each set a few times until it seems right to move on. Trying to count a specific number of "reps" will only distract you. You can visualize what the words mean or not. When your thoughts wander, just return gently to the exercise.

  Seeing my body being born, I breathe in;
  Smiling to my body being born, I breathe out.

  Seeing my cells living and dying, I breathe in;
  Smiling to my cells living and dying, I breathe out.

  Seeing my atoms in motion, I breathe in;
  Smiling to my atoms in motion, I breath out.

Seeing myself as an event, I breathe in.
Smiling to myself as an event, I breathe out.

Seeing my body returning to dust, I breathe in.
Smiling to my body returning to dust, I breathe out.

Then arise, go forth, and live your life. You'll be calmer, mentally sharper, and a bit less attached to the way things are. The five pairs of thoughts above are my own, provided as a starting place for you. Nhat Hanh has written many sets of these meditations, about all different aspects of life including emotions and healing. You'll find them in his wonderful, practical little book, *The Blooming of a Lotus.*

Listening Suggestions

Links to audio and video files are found at
www.livelikelouis.com.

"Heebie Jeebies" is described pretty well in the chapter, as is "Hello Dolly."

It surprised me to learn Pops had recorded John Lennon's "Give Peace a Chance." In my perfect world, someone is about to unearth a trove of unknown tapes of Louis doing an album's worth of Beatles songs. Barring that, we'll have to settle for this one, written by one of the lads Louis displaced in 1964. It's an odd record, really. On second thought, maybe it's better if those imaginary tapes remain buried.

Changing with the times also involved recording the title song for the James Bond film *On Her Majesty's Secret Service.* We get to hear Satchmo in a typical-sounding, late-sixties pop arrangement. This is the first recording made after a long hospital stay, but Louis sounds fine here, neither shaken nor stirred.

5   *Swing That Music*

*in which Louis and some high notes show us
we can be confident in our talents
and grow our gifts*

Ever pay someone a compliment and have them dismiss it? You say they did a good job, and they respond that anyone might have done as well. Or that it was "really nothing." Or that some part of it could have been better. Louis Armstrong on the other hand – though far from arrogant – was confident in his talent. He accepted his strengths, and this was one of the ingredients of his success in bringing joy to millions.

It was in late 1924 after the breakup of King Oliver's band in Chicago that Satchmo went to the Big Apple to be a featured player in the top black dance band there. But after a few weeks, he knew his talent wasn't being used to its full extent. He'd been singing all his life, and his new leader, Fletcher Henderson, really wasn't interested in what Louis had to offer that way. The few times Louis sang, it went over very well, but it never became part of the band's routine. Plus, Henderson limited Louis's cornet soloing to a few measures at a time. Though he was now in a premier band, Louis felt stifled. His wife, Lil, the college-educated piano player he had met in Oliver's band, was still in Chicago. She wrote to him that she had assembled a new group and wanted him to return and be its star. Louis hesitated. He maintained all his life that he hadn't wanted to be a star. But it meant better money. And his wife was, shall we say, a rather persuasive woman. She had been the driving force in Louis's leaving for New York in the first place. Now, with the opportunity for her husband to advance his (and her) fortunes even further by returning to Chicago, she sent him a pointed telegram: "Come by starting date or not at all."

Come he did.

And become a star, he did too. First in person, billed as "World's Greatest Cornet Player" on a huge sign (placed by his wife) he loathed. Then on record with his Hot Five discs selling out nationwide. In 1926 Louis was packing 'em in at the Dreamland club. Musicians were flocking to hear this phenom, enjoying his mastery and checking his horn to make sure his pyrotechnics weren't a trick. There was no trickery, just talent and hard work. Louis was nothing if not hardworking. For in addition to playing in nightclubs, he joined an orchestra that played in between the silent pictures at the Vendome Theater, the largest movie palace on Chicago's South Side. Here as on the riverboats, Louis played all kinds of music. But his special role was to be featured on the "hot" numbers. Leader Erskine Tate encouraged him to shine, even forcing him to go onstage lit by a spotlight. It was at the Vendome that Pops, always the entertainer, learned to use his trumpet's high range to thrill a crowd. He began his habit of repeating a high note 100 or more times. The audience would go wild, counting them all as he reeled them off. Then he'd slide up to an even higher note to end the piece and bring down the house. Later asked if he had been nervous about missing the note, Louis confidently replied, "I had it in my pocket all the time."

Negativity Comes Naturally

Not all are as confident in their abilities and accomplishments. Though American education and upbringing often teach children to assess their strengths and feel like winners (sometimes to extreme), many of us were taught that acknowledging our strengths was akin to bragging, and that we shouldn't think too much of ourselves. There is quite a contrast between the World War II generation, famous for humbly maintaining they were not heroes and only did what had to be done; and the mode now where every player gets a medal, and a B on a spelling test can be accompanied by a sticker proclaiming it "Awesome!" And yet there are still plenty of folks who would be hard pressed to acknowledge even a couple of strengths, or might feel it embarrassing or wrong to do so. But ask people where they're deficient or how they might improve, and stand back as the words start flowing. We're naturally attuned to negatives and deficiencies in general and we do not exclude ourselves. Psychiatrist David Burns calls our focusing on how we should be better a "shouldy" approach to life. (Say the word aloud to get the full effect of the pun.)

The former United Methodist bishop in Michigan, Rev. Donald Ott, once told a story of a young piano genius who walks offstage to wild applause after a concert. The custodian backstage remarks, "Listen to that, everyone's applauding." "No," the artist remarks glumly, "there's one who's not, way up in the balcony: my teacher." Bishop Ott remarked that very often we are that teacher, the one person disapproving of ourselves, even when others are appreciating what we've done or who we are. Even among our youth, where narcissism is measurably on the rise, there's still plenty of self-doubt to go around. I wish I had a free iTunes song credit for every time I've heard a high school Calculus student call herself dumb, or a student in Advanced Placement English declare himself bad at writing.

Psychologists tell us this is probably natural. Our ancient ancestors who noticed problems and dealt with them were more likely to survive and pass on their genes. If a band of cave-dwellers just sat around admiring their paintings and bearskin tunics, but failed to notice a hole in their defenses, they probably wouldn't survive too long. And so we inherit a survival strategy to notice deficiencies and not feel satisfied with good conditions. But life is beyond survival now. At least in the developed world with its social safety nets, physical survival is not really the issue. Now many of us have time and energy to use for personal growth and contributing to larger wholes, whether by taking piano lessons, reading to third-graders, or joining our local chapter of Ducks Unlimited. And when you're beyond true survival mode, the evidence is clear that it's far more effective to concentrate on, and develop, your strengths. Yet, we often continue to focus on our faults and (maybe) try to fix them. It's a hard instinct to fight. The great psychologist Carl Jung liked to remark, "You can throw nature out with a pitchfork, but she always comes back with a vengeance."

Strengths-Based Is Wiser

However, in spite of our instinct to attend to negatives, recognizing and developing strengths is a more efficient and productive avenue to success. Perhaps you've tried to eliminate a bad habit, or harder still, change a character trait you don't like. It *can* be done, but the time and energy required are monumentally greater than that needed to improve a strength. It's like trying to push a car stuck in the mud with the wheels pointing the wrong direction. Building on a strength, however, is like a cross-country skier giving herself a push in the direction she's already heading. *Far* less energy is required.

In addition to being more efficient, building on strengths is much more likely to be successful. New Year's resolutions are famous for lasting only a couple of weeks, though they *are* good for the gym membership industry. Isn't it natural to resist someone telling you what to do? So when trying to correct our faults, we become the nagging parent to ourselves. Of course, we'll then (non-consciously) resist our own bossy self and disobey: "I'll show 'me' who's boss: I *will* eat that donut!" Plus if you're looking to change a character trait, those become more difficult to change the longer you've spent being that way. This raises the likelihood of failure, giving yourself one more thing to feel bad about, creating a vicious circle. The "doom loop," Jim Collins, author of *Good to Great*, calls it. Building on strengths, however, leads to what Collins calls the "flywheel effect," a positive feedback loop. Using and growing a talent leads to success, which feels good and leads to wanting to grow your positives even more. Simply put, recognizing and building on strengths is far more efficient and far more productive than correcting faults.

I know how weird it can feel to let your faults be, trust me. Your biological and cultural programming will keep bringing shortcomings to mind, urging you to eliminate them, whether extra pounds, a messy desk, or being on the compulsive side. Your inner voice will whisper, "That's wrong; fix it." But research shows both in the personal sphere and in business if you were to choose exclusively either to build on strengths or correct faults, the one who attends to maximizing talents will end up further along. Collins even advocates, at least in business, finding the *one* thing you really do best and focusing your energy and effort on that single, distinctive service or ability.

Lest this seem too head-in-the sand, many ad-

vocates of strengths-based thinking will still tell you
if there is a fault truly sinking you, it must be addressed. If there's some hole in the boat causing you
to go under, yes, fix the hole rather than spiff up the
boat's nice paint job. We're talking literally about a
character trait or behavior that's harmful to yourself
or others. But most perceived weaknesses are not
dangerous, either literally or figuratively; usually
they're just annoying obsessions about how we
could improve, often in comparison to others. Imagine the owner of a cruise ship worrying that it's not
as nimble as a jet-ski, so she focuses on making it
more maneuverable while letting its wonderful cui-
sine go stale. Or imagine a jet-ski owner worried
that his agile little craft isn't swank like a cruise
ship, so he adds a champagne flute to the dash-
board. How much enjoyment would be lost, having
to trim speed so as not to spill the bubbly? These
are silly examples perhaps, but true in their essence:
it's smarter to spend your limited energy on knowing, accepting, and building on your strengths.
That's why strengths-based management, therapy,
and education are here to stay: not just fads, but
ideas whose time has come, thanks to their effi-
ciency and success.

Louis Armstrong was aware of his abilities. His
records sold out, the clubs were packed, people
screamed for him, early "hipsters" even adopted his
unique slang heard on some of the records. He later
(accurately) recollected that his bandleader in New
York hadn't recognized a million dollar talent when
he had one. But Louis never lorded it over anyone,
later thanking that leader for the opportunities he

did give him. Later, when he himself was a leader, Pops was known for being easy to work with and having a gracious spirit toward other musicians. On those Hot Five records where Louis started taking extended, fantastic solos, he let the other musicians solo too. Decades later the same would be true for the All Stars. When some critics noted the lesser abilities of some of the musicians who filled out his big bands in the 1930s and '40s, Louis remarked that if a player was trying, Pops could overlook the man's weaknesses to hear the good. He likened his philosophy to that of a churchgoer who enjoyed a good preacher, but could still look past a poor one to hear Jesus in the attempt. He wrote,

> I have played with quite a few musicians who weren't so good. But as long as they could hold their instruments correct, and display their willingness to play as best they could, I would look over their shoulder and see Joe Oliver and several other great masters from my home town.

1953: Louis continued to hit the high notes throughout his career, though more selectively.

Likewise, it's been my experience, working at entertainment venues and in education, to find that most who are truly excellent in their field do know it, but are not arrogant. Once, oddly enough, I met dancer/singer/actor/choreographer/director Gene Kelly alone in a university hallway. Our short encounter ended with *him* thanking *me* for appreciating his wonderful films. The tantrum-throwing diva gets all the press, but for each of them, there are many more who are aware that their talents are gifts on loan for the good of others. The best teachers I have known have always been generous in complimenting others and sharing their insights. Recognizing and focusing on your strengths clearly doesn't make you a self-centered jerk. One might even argue that to deny your strengths and focus on your weaknesses is itself a form of arrogance, devaluing the gifts you've been given. Didn't a famous Jewish rabbi even tell a parable about valuing and using your talents?

Your strengths are real. They are good. It's unwise, maybe even wrong, to ignore or dismiss them. Your strengths are the means by which you may most effectively cooperate with the ever-expanding spirit of growth and love. Your strengths are the means by which you can make ours a more wonderful world.

Practices

If you recognize yourself as someone who focuses on negatives, try this exercise. Make a list of some personal failings or weaknesses that bug you: unhelpful habits, good qualities you lack, or negative ones you possess.

Then – and this might feel odd – next to each fault write, "Let it be." As described above, it's counterintuitive not to want to eliminate a weakness. But accepting your weaknesses can allow you to focus more on your strengths. It can also make you more tolerant of your fellow human beings' shortcomings. Even if it feels wrong to admit a failing and abandon the need to fix it, write "Let it be" anyway.

Another exercise, involving movement: Hold your hands like a bowl and imagine your perceived faults in it. Then raise your arms and open the bowl, releasing the concerns upwards. Say this paraphrase of a well-known affirmation by author and teacher Wayne Dyer:

"I release the need to determine how I should be."

If you are religious, admit that if these perceived failings are to be "fixed" it is up to God to do so. Let go and let God, as the saying goes.

Notice that we are not so radical as to say your faults are good things or even okay (though you might come to see them that way). It is merely acknowledging that they are as they are, and it is far more efficient and beneficial to others to grow your strengths. Now try writing a few of these:

I give thanks for my talent/strength of . . .

I can grow it, by . . .

I can use it for good, by . . .

Listening Suggestions

Links to audio and video files are found at
www.livelikelouis.com.

It's time to encounter Louis's sheer trumpet virtuosity. Many critics and fans consider "West End Blues" from 1928 to be Louis's magnum opus. It even gets its own segment in Ken Burns' epic film, *Jazz*. Louis opens with an extended cadenza, a long, seemingly free-form solo. The trumpet traces its lineage back to war horns, and Louis in effect is sounding a bugle call to the world, "I am here. We are here." Toward the end of the piece, Pops holds a long note, then without taking a breath goes right into some groundbreaking musical creation and physical agility. Critic Gunther Schuller wrote, "The clarion call of 'West End Blues' served notice that jazz had the potential capacity to compete with the highest order of previously known musical expression." A true three-minute masterpiece, if ever there was one.

1927's "Potato Head Blues" is another piece with great, nimble, humorous playing. Behind Louis's solo the band provides a good example of "stop-time," the meaning of which will be self-evident when you listen.

To introduce "Swing That Music," the quintessential 1930s Satchmo showpiece, I must quote from biographer and archivist Ricky Riccardi's terrific blog, *The Wonderful World of Louis Armstrong* (www.dipperouth.blogspot.com):

> If you take blood pressure medication, take it before proceeding. If you have a bad back, now is a good time to strap yourself in tight to your chair. If you have bad breath, chew some gum, for heaven's sake. Okay, all ready, kids? Let's proceed with (drum roll please) "Swing That Music."

Here is Louis the Star Trumpeter strutting his stuff in 1936 on a song that would be thoroughly forgettable if not for Pops' marvelous trumpet work. Riccardi writes that it "displays his free-form sense of rhythm as it often floats above the frantic beat." During his last chorus you can hear Louis doing that thing he did to drive crowds wild, first in Chicago, then across the country and in Europe: a series of repeated high notes. In this case, for you musicians in the audience, it's forty-two concert high C's sliding up to a high E-flat for the finale.

Some critics think acclaim lured Louis away from the more creative solos of his 1920s recordings into a predictable rut of just belting out high notes. Notice, however, that he keeps them in his pocket for most of the record. Before them, his solo is really quite fluid, saving the repeated high C's for the ending. Louis was one star who knew what he was doing.

6 That's My Home

*in which Louis and his wife, Lucille,
remind us to appreciate our home*

In the late 1930s Louis got an extended gig playing
at the famous Cotton Club nightspot in Harlem.
One of the dancers, Lucille Wilson, caught his eye.
Louis found her very attractive, plus she seemed
very down-to-earth for someone in entertainment.
Here was a young woman with no real aspirations
to stardom, dancing only to support her mother and
siblings, even selling cookies to the entertainers
every evening. The smitten Louis started buying all
her cookies each night.

He decided to make a move. If you're ever in
need of a pick-up line, here's how Louis recalled
approaching Lucille. It doesn't get much more
straightforward than this: "Lucille, I might as well
tell you right now, I have eyes for you, and have
been having them for a long time. And if any of
these cats in the show [are] shooting at you, I want
to be in the running." It worked. The fact that Louis
was an extremely personable guy and a star entertainer probably didn't hurt either. After asking if

the Northern girl could cook red beans and rice, he invited himself over for dinner, ate "like a dog," and the courtship was on. They wed in 1942.

By that time, Louis had been away from his only home, New Orleans, for twenty years. He had lived in hotels and apartments. Lucille, however, didn't aspire to an entertainer's rambling existence, but to a stable middle-class life. Though she joined Louis on the road, living out of suitcases, it just wasn't to her tastes. At Christmastime she got an inkling that Louis himself would appreciate some stability. While Louis was on stage she set up a small tree in their hotel room. When he returned, Lucille recalled,

> he took one look at it and he just clammed up, you know? Louis isn't very emotional; he doesn't say much when he's overwhelmed. . . . We went to bed. And Louis was still laying up in bed watching the tree; his eyes just like a baby's eyes would watch something.

It was his first Christmas tree.

The next day, the band was due in another town, so Lucille was going to leave the tree. Louis, however, would have none of it. Lucille ended up carting the tree from hotel room to hotel room well into January. Louis even wanted it mailed home, and his wife had to convince him that was unworkable.

In 1943, after Lucille had returned to New York ahead of Louis, she went to the working-class Corona neighborhood of Queens. There she purchased a house from a white family she had known as a girl. It was a fairly imposing structure, two stories with a squared-off roofline, suggesting to my Midwestern eyes a segment of a townhouse. Architecture aside, there's a small twist in the tale: Lucille bought it without Louis's knowledge, giving him only an address to seek when done touring.

After many days on the road, Louis's band bus arrived in New York. He hired a cab and gave the cabbie the address. One long ride later, Louis arrived in the sedate, racially-mixed Queens neighborhood, a far cry from Harlem. He thought the cabbie either had gotten it wrong or was fooling him, but he was tired and in no mood for jokes. "One look at that big, *fine* house, and right away I said to the driver, 'Aw, man, quit kidding and take me to the address that I'm looking for.'" But he took a chance and went up to ring the doorbell. Who should open the door but Lucille in a silk nightie and curlers?

She showed him around the home she had bought and decorated. Louis loved the house, especially appreciating the care Lucille had put into furnishing it. "The more Lucille showed me around the house the more thrilled I got. . . . Right then I felt very grand all over it all. A little higher on the horse (as we express it). I've always appreciated the ordinary good things." After twenty years on the road, Louis had a real home.

He didn't spend too many days there at any one stretch until the last few years of his life. It was more Lucille's house than his, but Pops knew he had a home, a stable life awaiting him whenever he came off the road. In his later years, he loved being in his upstairs den listening to records and writing many long letters and personal essays there. On his state of the art tape recorders, he made 650 reel to reel tapes of readings, music, impromptu monologues, and discussions with friends. Then he would decorate the tape boxes in a fascinating collage style using photos, clippings, and other bits and pieces. In the 1950s Louis even collaged-over the walls in his den. Unfortunately, the ever-tasteful Lucille had them removed.

You can actually visit Louis's inner sanctum and soak up some Satchmo karma. His beloved house is not only still there, it's a wonderful museum, operated by Queens College. It's restored to look just as it did when Louis and Lucille lived there, including a turquoise "kitchen of the future" and a gold-fixtured bathroom featured on the show "Lifestyles of the Rich and Famous."

But no matter how fine and decorated it might be, a house is not a home. That takes people and the life they live together. Though Louis had three wives before Lucille, the fourth time was the charm. Louis and Lucille stayed together 'til Louis's death parted them in 1971. Louis wrote in a private letter,

> I love my wife, Lucille + she loves me. Or else we wouldn't have been together this long. Especially doing the crazy things I usually do for kicks. That's why I love her, because she's smart. The average woman would have quit my ol' ass – long, long ago.

Lucille was in her twenties when they were wed, but the Armstrongs never had children of their own. This was not through any lack of trying, if we believe Louis's many candid remarks about their love life. Louis did have an adopted son, though. When he was fourteen Louis had taken it upon himself to support his sick cousin, Flora, who had been taken advantage of by an older white man. Louis and his relatives were unable to afford the doctor's two-dollar fee. Flora died, but not before entrusting her baby to Louis's care by naming the child Clarence Armstrong.

Louis took his duties very seriously. At age seventeen when he married for the first time, he adopted Clarence, too. Clarence was mentally handicapped, which Louis blamed on a fall off a high, wet porch when he was three. Nevertheless, when he moved to Chicago Louis sent for Clarence and raised him, keeping Clarence with him as he went through two more marriages. Eventually Clarence was installed in a home of his own in the Bronx, which Louis visited often.

Home Includes the Neighborhood

Louis spent most of his life on the road until his last years. But he and Lucille were still an integral part of their Queens neighborhood for decades. Louis wrote in 1970 how Lucille would roast a turkey or ham for neighbors when there was a death, and how he enjoyed walking two blocks to Joe's Artistic Barber Shop for a trim. Dinner at his favorite Chinese restaurant would often grow cold due to the number of autographs he'd sign for neighbor kids. Those children were very important. He wrote,

> During my 54 years traveling on the road playing one night stands, and when I would return home, all of those kids in my block would be standing there right in front of my door waiting to help me unload my luggage and take it into the house.

Close friend Phoebe Jacobs recounts how when Louis came home off the road, "very often the neighbors would have banners out, 'Welcome Home, Pops.'" On nice days "he'd sit on the front steps of his house and buy kids Good Humors. And he'd ask them, 'Was your homework good? Were you a good boy?'"

Pops had a little balcony off his den and would play his horn there in the evening. If a couple of days went by without hearing his trumpet, neighbors would call and ask about his health. Lucille would let them know he was merely occupied with other matters. Once when his health truly wasn't good, after being released from the hospital with heart problems, neighborhood adults and children alike were careful to be quiet in the vicinity of the Armstrong residence. Their respect made quite an impression on Louis.

In the 1950s and '60s, Louis went from being a star to being an American institution. Lucille and his manager tried to get him to move, either to a bigger house in a neighborhood outside the city, or out to sunny Los Angeles, capital of the entertainment biz. Louis was adamant: he would not be moved. The home in Queens was fine enough for him, and he wasn't one to put on airs:

> We don't need to move out in the suburbs to some big mansion. . . . What for? What the hell I care about living in a "fashionable" neighborhood? Ain't nobody cuttin' off the lights and gas here 'cause we didn't pay our bills. The Frigidaire is full of food. What more do we need?

Plus, he treasured the specific connections he had made with the people in his neighborhood. Why cut those ties just for a "nicer" address and swimming pool? Pops remarked,

> We've both seen three generations grow up in our block where we bought our home in Corona, white and black, and those kids when they grew up and got married – their children – still come around to our house and visit their Uncle Louis and Aunt Lucille.

The regard people in his "Elmcor" neighborhood had for Louis is seen in a very touching photograph taken just after his death. A group of Little Leaguers holds homemade signs reading "Elmcor loves you," "Elmcor will never forget our Louie," and "Satchmo will live forever in our community."

Wanting What You Have

True confession time: these stories about Lucille, Louis, their home, and how he treasured it are the tales from this book I most need to hear. Not that I don't need the reminders we find in the other chapters. But valuing my home and family comes hard to me. In fact as I write this, it's summer vacation for us teacher-types, and where am I? At school, writing. Why? It's quiet. You see, I'm an introvert who likes calm and order. At my relatively small house are three teenagers, their friends, their stuff, two cats, and a dog: not exactly the recipe for calm and order. More like *The Family Circus.*

When the noise and clutter get to me, I find myself obsessing about what's wrong, rather than seeing and hearing what's right. I get to feeling like Jimmy Stewart's character, George Bailey, in the classic film *It's a Wonderful Life*, when he comes home in a dark mood. One kid is practicing the same song over and over on the piano, another is asking him how to spell some word, one is upstairs with a cold, and the little one keeps following him around saying, "'Scuze me." All that (plus his *really* bad day at work) makes him flip out. I know you've seen it: he yells at the kids and smashes a model of a bridge that's symbolic of his unrealized dreams of doing big things. Luckily George gets enlightened (by an angel named Clarence, ironically) and comes to see everything in a new light. Instead of bridges and fame, he enjoys a loving wife, decent kids, a roof over his head, and a town full of friends. He ends up wanting what he already has, which is a pretty sure recipe for real and lasting happiness.

Nicolas Cage portrays a man in a similar situation in *Family Man*. His character is a well-off single guy who wakes up in an alternate future, with kids bouncing on his bed in suburban Jersey. Though he initially wants his old single life back, he comes to appreciate the love that comes with the chaos. Some days I feel like *I* could use a visit from an angel to see what I'd be missing if life had turned out differently. I'll settle instead for the extended stay I'm getting with Satchmo and try to remember to use the practices at the end of this chapter.

I'm mindful that you who are reading this may be in a different situation, but still not treasuring your home. Perhaps your household feels not too noisy, but too empty. Or your apartment is too small, or your town is not to your liking. I would urge you, as I urge myself, to look on the positives that *are* there if we'll only have eyes and ears for them. Peace and quiet can give you important room to think or create or volunteer. Louis and Lucille were childless, but took it as an opportunity to bless many children in their neighborhood. A difficult neighbor or neighborhood can be an opportunity for prayer or service.

Very often no situation is absolute, but what we make of it. As Hamlet observes, there is nothing either good or bad but thinking makes it so. The Hebrew scriptures even tell us that as we think, so we are. The apostle Paul instructed a group of early Greek Christians that their life would be enhanced if they would see and focus on the good: "Whatsoever things are true, whatsoever things are honest, whatsoever things are just, whatsoever things are pure, whatsoever things are lovely, whatsoever things are of good report; if there be any virtue, and if there be any praise, think on these things." May you and I look for and think on whatever is good about our homes. Just like Louis.

Practices

Our attention is essentially a one-track system. While we are consciously focusing on the positive, we cannot – at that moment, anyway – be thinking of the negative. And since our thoughts and feelings interconnect, while we focus our thoughts on the positive we'll also feel better.

Take a few moments and jot down five things that could be viewed as good about your home or living situation. Write things about your household, family, dwelling, neighborhood, whatever. Bad things that aren't present also count (for example, "Our roof doesn't leak anymore").

If you get stuck for positives, acknowledge a negative feeling you presently have – no harm in being honest – then write a way it could be worse: "My house may be cramped . . . but at least the roof doesn't leak anymore." Or, "The dog is annoying to me . . . but she doesn't chew on my stuff."

If appreciating what you have is as difficult for you as it often is for me, remembering and writing your blessings will help you want what you already have. Try doing it several days in a row. You can expand it to other areas of negativity (if you have them) and make it a part of your morning routine. The repetition can even retrain your mind. What brain researcher Dr. Daniel Amen calls ANTs (automatic negative thoughts) can eventually be exterminated, replaced by positive thoughts.

Extra Credit

1. Buy an old 78 record of Louis's "That's My Home" via Ebay.

2. Hang it in a prominent place near your front door so you see it as you enter.

3. See how it affects you.

Yes, your author actually did this, and frankly, on its own, seeing the record every day didn't affect me much. But it looks cool and has started a number of conversations with guests wondering why I have an old Satchmo record hanging on the wall. Discussing Louis Armstrong can't help but raise a home's happiness quotient, right?

Listening Suggestions

Links to audio and video files are found at
www.livelikelouis.com.

I've seen "That's My Home" described as "saccha-
rine" and I suppose it is. But Louis's 1932 recording
of it is very moving, an example of his ability to
transcend and transform the material he often had
to work with. His friend and long-time bassist, Arvell Shaw, heard Louis's real self coming through
every time Satchmo performed this number, one of
his most requested tunes: "I listened not so much to
the timbre of the voice, but to the *feeling*, because it
was something that went deep inside. . . . When he
would sing, 'I'm always welcomed back, no matter
where I roam; it's just a little shack, to me it's home
sweet home,' so help me I'd have to fight back the
tears. Now *every night* we'd do that!"

Louis and Clarence

A friend advised me not to use specific website
sources for these listening examples. But if there's
any justice in the universe, Ricky Riccardi's aforementioned blog (dippermouth.blogspot.com) will
be with us a long, long time. If anything ever qualified as a treasure trove, it's Ricky's blog: in-depth
articles on Satchmo's recordings and life, with

countless rare recordings and video clips. If you access it and search for the June 15, 2008 (Father's Day) entry, you'll be rewarded with an audio clip from a very early TV show featuring Louis and his son, Clarence. Ricky is right, in his observation that Louis's pride and love for Clarence come shining through, even in a one-minute exchange.

7 It's a Most Unusual Day

*in which Louis and a certain product
remind us to be ourselves
and not worry too much what others think*

We've gone six chapters without acknowledging a serious fact about Louis Armstrong. It's time to face the music: Louis was an addict. Yes, an addict . . . to an herbal remedy named Swiss Kriss: in short – a laxative. A *very* strong laxative. Louis's relationship to his beloved Swiss Kriss, and his evangelistic zeal in promoting it, can help us remember to relax and care a bit less what other people think of us.

Louis had been raised as many people were in his day to take a regular dose of "physic" in order to stay a "regular fellow." His mother, Mayann, trained him and his sister to do this at an early age. Louis recalled Mayann instructing them that because of "the food that you all eat today, you must take a good purge and clean your little stomachs out thoroughly. They will keep the germs away." Louis and his sistrer "both gave Mayann our word that we would stay physic-minded for the rest of our lives."

And so he did. In 1918 Louis did not succumb to the Spanish flu pandemic, but helped take care of the people in his neighborhood who were ill. He attributed his immunity to being "physic-minded" and taking that weekly dose of laxative. Given the lack of sanitation and refrigeration back then, who knows? Maybe he was right.

Louis writes about laxatives in his autobiography five times, which might seem odd. (It seemed so to me, frankly.) In fact, it might seem odd for someone to write about laxatives even once. Another perspective, however, is to remember what a normal part of life going to the bathroom is, and acknowledge that Louis had no problem writing about this natural function. In his many preserved letters and interviews, he discusses everything, all aspects of life: food, music, sex, sleep, health, and yes, bowel movements. I get the feeling that he was very natural in the sense that life was whole and integrated for him – it was not segmented and partitioned, with some topics off-limits.

He certainly had no trouble promoting Swiss Kriss. It's an herbal concoction still available even in my small city's only health food store. He discovered it in the writings of a health guru in the 1950s. The ingredients reminded him of the herbs his mother picked in New Orleans to clean out her children's systems. So he switched to it from his long-time purgative, Pluto Water (a lovely concoction whose ads featured the devil and the slogan, "When nature won't, Pluto will!"). Like many converts, he became something of a fanatic and gave out little packets of the highly effective Swiss Kriss to everyone he met, from friends to fellow musicians to audience members to diplomats, even to his nurses when he was hospitalized near the end of his life. He was especially happy he convinced the head nurse to try it, referring to her as "one of my toughest customers."

He often talked and wrote about Swiss Kriss, once proclaiming, "I take my Swiss Kriss, man, they keep you rollin'. Old Methuselah, he'd have been here with us if he had known about them." In a printed flyer to promote his diet methods, he gave instructions for getting started on Swiss Kriss.

> Your first dose will be real heavy to start blasting right away, and get the ball to rolling. . . . Don't get frantic because you have to trot to the bathroom several times when you first get up (awakened). P.S. You won't need an alarm clock to awaken you, no-o-o-o. . . . When you and Swiss Kriss get well acquainted, then you'll dig he's your friend.

He later jokes that if Swiss Kriss sponsors a radio show for him, his opening will be, "This is Satchmo speaking for Swiss Kriss. Are you loosening?"

Louis even had himself photographed on the toilet with the picture cropped to appear as if we're seeing him through a keyhole. (His bare behind is just barely hidden.) Beneath the photo he attached a prominent "Satchmo-slogan" urging folks to "leave it all behind ya," and had hundreds of promotional copies printed up. Another of his favorite slogans (appropriate for a horn player) was "Keep blasting!" and he often signed his letters "Swiss Krissly yours." (Ironically, his other common signature referred to his favorite food: "Red beans and ricely yours.") One story has a musician in a taxi-cab trying to smoke Swiss Kriss, since Pops had told him the herbs were such good stuff!

Tony Bennett enjoys telling the story of being at a dinner with Louis Armstrong and members of the British royal family including Princess Alexandra and the Duke of Kent. Amid discussion after a sumptuous meal, the princess turns to Tony and asks, "Did you ever try this?" She's holding a packet of Swiss Kriss. Louis had distributed "this very ferocious laxative" to the royal family! As Bennett tells it, the royals start reading the instructions, realize what it is, and the entire dinner party cracks up with people falling on the floor from laughter. He describes the mayhem as "the funniest thing I've actually seen, funnier than any Laurel and Hardy scene."

Please note that Louis didn't go around recommending a laxative just to shock people. Being rude to people was not his style. He sincerely thought Swiss Kriss was good for you. He wanted you to know about it, so he'd tell you. He didn't care if some people might think it crude. With Louis, what you saw was what you got. For example, when he returned as a star to New Orleans in 1931, a white announcer refused to introduce a "colored" band on the radio. Louis grabbed the mike and did it himself. Playing for King George in England, he ignored protocol and acknowledged the royal presence, lightheartedly announcing a brief solo, "This one's for you, Rex." After shows, in his dressing room he would receive everyone from the local mayor to old friends from New Orleans wanting a handout, with Louis dressed in his underwear with a kerchief on his head. He addressed President Eisenhower as "Daddy" and was the same around the Pope as he was around his friends. In fact, a story circulated after Louis met the Pope in the 1960s: the pontiff asks if Louis and his wife have children. Louis replies, "No, Dad, but we're still wailin'."

Satchmo was thoroughly comfortable with who he was, the same person no matter his surroundings. He could easily have echoed the catchphrase of another great star of the thirties, a certain spinach-eating sailor man who often stated, "I yam what I yam."

Pops in his kerchief, backstage at the Aquarium, New York, 1946.

You can do less, well.

There's a lesson here for me because I have too often worried what other people think. I do realize it's
natural to care what others think about us. We're
social animals, so we're hard-wired to care about
the esteem of others. Primitive people who had
more support were more likely to survive and pass
on their genes. And in no way am I saying that we
should be inconsiderate of others' feelings.   But
worry a *bit* less about what other people might
think of us? Good call.

One way caring too much about others' opinions can show itself is by taking on tasks you feel
you "should" do, shouldering duties you imagine a
"good person" would undertake, even if they're
really not right for you. It might be serving on a
committee, joining a community group, even doing
things for your family. Service is very good, but can
be over-done for the wrong reason, because you feel
you "ought." This overextension often comes from
caring about what others think, trying to fit some
image of the "good" mother or son or employee or
citizen. It seems especially tough for women to resist this; thanks to the hormone oxytocin, you female folk are generally more prone to be nurturing
and attuned to others' needs. Plus, our culture tells
each woman she should be a sexy wife, the world's
best mom, and a success in her career, all at the
same time!

I hope by this point in the book you can trust
that I would never say we shouldn't do things for
others; nor should we avoid clear matters of duty or

necessity. Contributing to the well-being of others is the essence of a meaningful life. But taking on *too* much, for the wrong reasons, then burning out or being resentful does little good and possibly much harm. If you're like me, you know this, but still need to be reminded it's okay to say no to things. Rarely will people think less of you. And if they do, adopt a bit of the Satchmo attitude: Let 'em!

Recently I resigned from a faculty committee. I explained to my principal that I supported the group's focus, but it wasn't one I was passionate about. I told him that to be most productive I need to spend my energy in areas I'm truly enthused about. Not only did he understand (high school principals definitely understand about being pulled in too many directions), he commended my decision. I was putting into practice a phrase I learned several years ago, but which has really stuck with me: "Do less, well." It makes for a saner, more centered life, one not so much in the "spin cycle." The philosopher Thoreau advised us,

> Our life is frittered away by detail. Simplify, simplify, simplify! I say, let your affairs be as two or three, and not a hundred or a thousand; instead of a million count half a dozen, and keep your accounts on your thumb-nail.

When you simplify, you're more able to be one with life and serve others from the center – instead of just adding one more spinning plate or juggling ball to an already confusing mix.

But can you wear purple?

Caring too much about others' opinions can also result in avoiding doing things they might think odd. Again, this is very normal, but also stifling. I'm reminded of the poem "Warning," by Jenny Joseph. It inspired the Red Hat Society, that international organization of daring grannies. The speaker in the poem begins by warning hearers that when she is old she will wear purple. But why wait until then? I suppose if you're in the corporate world, it could hold back your career if you wore a purple suit. But certainly in your off hours you could go for it. Let "purple" stand for whatever people might think is a bit goofy or daft (for instance, say, talking about a laxative all the time or wearing a kerchief on your head in your dressing room).

That spirit of cutting loose and not caring so much about others' opinions is probably why the BBC found Ms. Jones' poem to be the United Kingdom's most popular post-war poem in a 1996 poll. Learning that the poem is of British origin really didn't surprise me, since the English are known for allowing themselves to be a bit eccentric, indulging in somewhat odd hobbies and tastes. We driven Americans could probably learn something. Even Star Trek fans.

You see, I am one of those, a Trekkie dating back to my babyhood in the late '60s. No, I can't recite Shakespeare or the Bible in the Klingon language as some fans can; but I have gone to a couple of conventions and dressed in a Star Trek uniform for the movie premiere in 2009. After the movie was out for a while, a discussion thread was started in an online Trek forum, asking if we fans were now wearing Star Trek shirts in public. Not costumes, mind you, just t-shirts. Many respondents replied that they still were not, concerned what people would think or say. Of all the people in the world, you'd think *Trekkies* wouldn't care what people think, right? But the urge not to stand out runs deep.

After reading that thread I promptly went and found one of my Trek shirts, and a great one at that: four pictures of Mr. Spock arranged a la Andy Warhol. I threw it on and, since it was summer, took my ten-year-old son to the beach. We parked near the skateboard area full of "cool" nonconformist kids all wearing similar black clothing in the hot sun. Right away, deep from the primitive regions of my brain, came bubbling up a feeling of being . . . conspicuous. I was a middle-aged man instantly transported back to 1979 in junior high wearing an uncool shirt. As I walked my son toward the beach, two arriving skateboarders passed us. One quietly said, "Nice shirt." She probably meant it, since the movie was popular and still fresh in people's minds. But I was far from sure at the time.

Not only did I feel conspicuous, I felt guilty about it, for I had set out deliberately to be myself and not care what others thought. Emotions are complicated. I should add that walking past beautiful and/or buff sunbathers didn't help me feel any cooler sporting my Spock shirt. It was a good experience, though – it reminded me how strong is the urge not to stick out, a power that can stifle you from being yourself. I do, after all, like Star Trek; I've never really been a "cool" guy anyway and I need to remember that's okay – and just enjoy being what I "yam."

I think I can safely assume that you, O reader, are not a Swiss Kriss devotee. And it's unlikely you're a fellow Trekkie. But I'll bet there *is* some quirk about you, a weird hobby or a certain style you might like to wear that's not exactly, shall we say . . . up to date. Maybe you just have a penchant for singing loudly while you do housework or eat a snack your family finds bizarre. You can follow Louis's example, disregard what people think, and be who you are.

Our world will be a bit more wonderfully purple for it.

Practices

Swiss Kriss Directions for Musicians

Found on the Liberty Hall Jazz Quartet's website, these directions seem to come authentically from Satchmo's fertile mind. For the life of me, however, I cannot track down the original source. Use at your own risk therefore; I am not a doctor, nor do I play one on TV!

    1. All Musicians: One tablet (1 tspn. fiber) before dawn;
    2. Big Band Leaders: An extra dose 1 hour before performance;
    3. Featured Vocalists: An extra dose 15 minutes before performance.

You can eliminate a stressor.

It's all right, even *good*, to do less. If you are in too many optional activities, you can give yourself permission to seek a calmer, more efficient life. Then explain it to whoever is in charge in those terms, that you simply need fewer doings in order to be better at what you stay doing. Most people are understanding (sometimes even a little envious) of someone with the courage to check out of the spin cycle.

You can wear purple.

Whatever is your purple, let me urge you to identify and "wear" it today. Even if it's a Spock shirt to the beach. Enjoy.

Listening Suggestions

Links to audio and video files are found at
www.livelikelouis.com.

"Mahogany Hall Stomp" is a very nice tune with a melody and solo once commonly memorized by jazz trumpet players. Mahogany Hall was a legendary brothel in New Orleans, which brings up one last thing about Louis's personality he didn't hide. He liked prostitutes. Not as a customer, just as a fellow human being. He had delivered coal to them as a boy, lived in a red-light district, even made a prostitute his first wife. So when on tour, especially in the South, he welcomed them into his dressing room along with everybody else, the local dignitaries, the hustlers, the ministers, everyone, and he made it clear they were welcome. He often gave them help. If anyone had a problem with that, so be it. Louis loved people, and prostitutes were people too.

8   *Black and Blue*

*in which Louis and a president show us
we can be courageous*

In our first chapter, we accompany the five-year-old
Louis Armstrong as he first meets Jim Crow on a
segregated streetcar in 1906. Segregation continued,
of course, and now we jump forward about fifty
years to an incident in which Louis willingly jeop-
ardizes his career to fight ongoing discrimination.
Through his bravery this man shows us that we too
can act with courage when it comes time to take a
stand.

The Race Situation in 1957

This is not the place for an in-depth retelling of the
history of Jim Crow laws. They're familiar to most
Americans, either through history class or life experience. We know of the separate (and substandard)
drinking fountains, beaches, hospitals, and schools.
Most harmful was the fact that those who were kept
down were barred from voting due to literacy tests

and poll taxes. They could not begin to change the rules that held them back. In the 1940s blacks went off to Europe to defeat Hitler's brand of racial superiority only to return and find America's version still going strong. In some ways, by the early fifties not much had changed since little Louis's streetcar ride.

We've seen how Satchmo was open to white musicians and how he dared to form and maintain an integrated band starting in 1947. But by no means was his head in the sand regarding the difficult state of race relations in his country. Writing near the end of his life, he recollected how sometimes in his childhood days, whites would get drunk and go hunting for a black man to shoot – *any* black man.

> They wouldn't give up until they found one. From then on, Lord have mercy on the poor darkie. Then they would torture the poor darkie, as innocent as he may be. They would get their usual ignorant Chess Cat laughs before they would shoot him down – like a dog. My, my, my, those were the days.

No matter his fame or status, no black man was immune to discrimination. Even in the North, Louis played in plenty of whites-only nightclubs. On tour in the South, segregated lodgings were the rule. During his triumphant return to New Orleans in 1931 he tried to host a dance at an army base for his black hometown fans, but was prevented at the last minute due to race. By the late 1950s, Pops had met

the Pope, toured Europe and Japan, dined with
royalty, and played for a crowd of 100,000 in
Ghana. But he couldn't play in New Orleans. A new
Jim Crow law there prohibited performances by
integrated bands. In an interview, he described his
feelings towards his hometown:

> I ain't goin' back to New Orleans and let
> them white folks in my own hometown be
> whipping on me and killing me for my hus-
> tle. . . . Ain't it stupid? Jazz was born in
> New Orleans. . . . And I can remember
> when it wasn't no crime for cats of any color
> to get together and blow. They treat me bet-
> ter all over the world than they do in my
> own hometown.

"I don't care if I never see New Orleans again,"
he declared. He kept his word, staying away until
1965 after passage of the federal Civil Rights Act.
New Orleans is evidence now of how far we've
come since then. If you're fortunate enough to take
a plane flight to New Orleans, first off, your seat
won't be assigned to you based on the color of your
skin. Second, the airport where you'll land is named
for a black man: the Louis Armstrong New Orleans
International Airport! But in 1957 such progress
was only just beginning.

As you probably know, in that year one of the
most important skirmishes in the long fight for progress occurred in Little Rock, Arkansas. You might
not know the school board had in fact voted to inte-
grate the schools. But Gov. Orville Faubus couldn't

bear to see that happen. He deployed the Arkansas National Guard to block the path of nine black students trying to attend Central High School. He was clearly violating the Supreme Court's *Brown v. Board* decision and the authority of the federal government. President Eisenhower expressed his displeasure. Nevertheless, the national guard troops stood for days in front of the school, barring the door to education and equal protection of the laws. Some residents joined them to scream and spit at the teens. Others held prayer services for peace. The whole country was watching, including citizen Louis Armstrong. After a lifetime of discrimination, enough was enough.

Why the Risk Was Great

Before we examine the action Louis took, we need to understand that it was indeed a risk. Accustomed as we are to celebrities sounding off on social issues today, this was not the norm then. Sports stars and entertainers stuck to their trade and generally kept their mouths shut. Partly this was just the times, and partly it was sage business practice not to alienate a segment of one's audience. By 1957 Louis's audience was mainly white.

In the 1920s his records had been devoured by blacks. His in-your-face, bravura style of playing had made him a hero for many, a fellow black who was making it in the whites' world. "There was something in that voice they appreciated, the pride of race," observed blues composer W.C. Handy.

People throughout Chicago's South Side and Harlem even started talking like him, learning his special lingo from the vocals and spoken-word portions of his many hit records.

But times change, and to younger black Americans of the postwar era, Louis seemed like a relic of a past they were trying to forget. Their tastes were moving on to early rhythm and blues on the pop side, and frenetic, intellectual "be-bop" on the jazz side. White tastes were moving his way, however. By the 1950s Louis's accessible, happy music had made him white peoples' favorite "Negro." A huge crossover star, he had been appearing in movies for years and had begun doing the myriad television appearances that would make him universally known. So, to speak up about racial injustice could cost him plenty in those very tense times, a period we often incorrectly remember as bland "happy days." In the paranoid aftermath of McCarthyism, at the height of the Cold War and in the midst of civil rights protests and backlash, it was quite a risky move for Louis to speak up. But seeing soldiers denying black children a fair education was the last straw.

What He Said

Louis was on tour in North Dakota in 1957, ironically the first black ever to stay in the Dakota hotel in Grand Forks. A young reporter disguised as a waiter snuck into his room. Louis warmed to the young man's gutsiness and opened up. It was not an unplanned outburst to be retracted later. Louis even signed off on the reporter's transcript of their conversation. He would not use the excuse – as public figures so often do now – that his words were taken out of context. His deliberate remarks were distributed by the Associated Press and printed in papers across the country:

> Mr. Armstrong said President Eisenhower had "no guts" and described Gov. Orval E. Faubus of Arkansas as an "uneducated plow boy." He said the President was "two-faced" and had allowed Governor Faubus to run the Federal Government. "It's getting almost so bad a colored man hasn't got any coun-try," the Negro entertainer said.

We now know these strong words were even stronger in the original and cleaned up for the pa-pers. The reporter, Larry Lubnow, has discussed their conversation in that hotel room, and suffice it to say that Louis called Gov. Faubus something considerably worse than a "plow boy." When asked about a planned tour of Russia for the U.S. State Department, Louis replied, "The way they are treat-ing my people in the South, the Government can go to hell."

Reaction, as they say, was mixed. Jackie Robin-son came forward to echo Pops' criticism of Eisenhower, while Sammy Davis, Jr., chided Louis for not speaking out earlier. Columnist Jim Bishop called Louis an "ingrate," and the University of Alabama cancelled a planned concert. President

Eisenhower didn't respond to Armstrong. He did respond to Faubus, however, with the presence of the 101st Army Airborne division to escort the Little Rock Nine to class. Louis, in turn, responded with some "class" of his own in a personal telegram to the president:

> Mr. President. Daddy if and when you decide to take those little negro children personally into Central High School along with your marvelous troops, please take me along[.] "O God it would be such a great pleasure I assure you." . . . You have a good heart. . . . Am Swiss Krissly yours Louis Satchmo Armstrong.

It turns out Louis's career did not suffer too adversely, though it certainly might have. Such had happened to Paul Robeson, the great black actor and singer who had criticized the United States and compared it unfavorably to the Soviet Union. Blacklisting was a fact of life in the 1950s, a major fear of entertainers. Nevertheless, as Louis put it several days after his initial comment, "When I see on television and read about a crowd spitting on and cursing at a little colored girl . . . I think I have a right to get sore and say something about it."

Opportunities for Courage, Here in Zombie Land

Fast forward from 1957 to now. Where are the opportunities for courage? In an interesting essay for the *New York Times*, Chuck Klosterman perceived that so many books and movies are featuring zombies lately because they stand for what we fear about ourselves: that we are wage-enslaved, cubicle-imprisoned drones. We appear fully human, but are really just . . . zombies. Compared to our ancestors who lived lives fraught with real danger, whether from beasts or invaders, most of us do lead fairly safe lives. Not to say we don't have hardships and discouragements, but our lives just don't seem to call for real courage as much as our ancestors' did. Maybe this is a misperception on our part. Generations often feel they've gone soft compared to their rugged forebears. Even Teddy Roosevelt's generation in the 1890s felt that way, comparing itself unfavorably to the "manly" Civil War generation that preceded it.

So maybe it's a case of rose-colored glasses in reverse, but it sure seems true: leaving my "hut" every morning to go motivate eleventh-graders to learn about civics is simply not as dangerous as going off to hunt a wildebeest or defend the village from the enemies across the bay. An essential element of humanity is courage. Where can you be courageous these days?

In our lives there are still things that need doing, in both the personal domain and the larger, social sphere. Usually the cost is time and effort, which equate to "work" or "perseverance," certainly good things. But sometimes the doing also involves risk. *Now* you're talking "courage." Louis Armstrong thought soldiers preventing kids from being treated like human beings had to stop. What he could offer were words. Those words could have cost him considerable standing and income. He deliberately spoke them anyway. Courage.

Here are a few instances where courage might be called for, even in our modern, somewhat zombified era:

To say no to your child can risk making him or her mad at you for a time.

To tell the boss that a proposed decision isn't wise can risk being on the outs or considered "not a team player."

To speak up about a public policy can risk friends and relatives disliking you (or even unfriending you on Facebook, as a friend of mine discovered).

To share something about your past, or about struggles you go through, can risk people thinking less of you or even using that knowledge against you.

Yet, as Stephen King marvelously puts it, "There is no gain without risk, perhaps no risk without love."

But How to Actually Do the Courageous Thing?

Ay, there's the rub. Some situations can still involve risk in doing something that needs to be done. But how to actually *do* that courageous act? Our fear of negative consequences is always there urging us not to speak or act. We're hard-wired to want acceptance from the group. And the risk of losing a job, or even just one's status within the company, plays on our deep-seated, biological fear of a lack of resources for the future. So in light of these very natural concerns, how can you be brave?

First, you can remember and reflect on others who were brave. What we feed our minds affects our behaviors. You can read stories from your faith, events where a woman or man faces risks but shows courage to accomplish some good. You can also recall people from history who risked greatly for social change or the good of others.

Second, you can think about the importance of the act that is called for. If it's standing firm as a parent, you can consider how important it is for your children to develop into mature, responsible adults. If it's speaking up at work, you can remember that the well-being of the company is important not just to yourself, but to all its employees and the communities it affects. If it's sharing something about yourself, think of the potential benefit to the person you'll open up to. If it's standing by someone in a trying time, consider the importance of your loyalty to him or her.

In other words, focus on the need for the deed. Civil rights leader Cesar Chavez focused on the importance of helping people have decent living conditions: "It is my deepest belief that only by giving life do we find life, that the truest act of courage, the strongest act of manliness is to sacrifice ourselves for others in a totally non-violent struggle for justice. To be a man is to suffer for others. God help us to be men."

Third, you can acknowledge that brave people do feel fear. Mark Twain aptly wrote, "Courage is resistance to fear, mastery of fear – not absence of fear. Except a creature be part coward it is not a compliment to say it is brave." Gen. George Patton admitted candidly that all men feel fear in battle, but courage "is fear holding on a minute longer." Former Navy SEAL Howard Wasdin, commenting on the mission to capture Osama bin Laden said, "The difference between being afraid and a warrior is controlling that fear and using it as a tool in accomplishing the mission."

Finally, you can find others to be brave with. Does it seem to lessen the bravery if the deed is shared? Perhaps it does in our modern minds, formed as they are in our highly individualistic culture. But recall that even the Lone Ranger was far from alone (and many times it was Tonto who really saved the day). The Hebrew patriarch Abraham left Ur to find the Promised Land not alone, but with his extended family. Jesus deliberately set his face towards Jerusalem and crucifixion, in the company of twelve friends. George Washington didn't fight the British without an army. In fact in that conflict, old Ben Franklin remarked, "We must all hang together or assuredly we shall all hang separately." And it was with her friends and colleagues that Alice Paul risked freedom and health for women's suffrage. If the company of others dilutes the bravery, then most of our heroes just got disqualified.

Modern research shows that a social element actually is often an important part of bravery. Social psychologists have investigated why bystanders sometimes look on and do nothing when witnessing an assault, while at other times people will intervene. One important factor for intervening is seeing someone else act first. That first (*very* brave) person shows other potential helpers hanging back that they will have an ally in the fight. This breaks the ice of anonymity and can even transform a crowd of onlookers into a band of helpers. So if you feel a situation calls for bravery, find an ally, and more than one if possible. You will feel more free to be courageous (and your chances for success improve, too). As the Hebrew proverb tells us, "if an attacker prevails against one, two shall withstand him; and a threefold cord is not quickly broken."

Note that it was 1957 in which Louis spoke up about segregation. Conditions were as bad or worse in 1927 or '37, but people speaking up then was far more rare. In the 1950s, however, the Movement was afoot. Many other people, black and white, were speaking up and taking action then. The risks to his career were still just as real as if he had been alone, but the existence of potential allies probably played a part in Pops taking his stand when he did.

Now is a different era, but just as in Louis Armstrong's day, there will be moments that arise in your life where right action risks loss. To echo Cesar Chavez, in those times may you not shrink back as an onlooker, but step forward and act as a true man or woman.

Practices

As discussed earlier, one way to have an inner reserve of courage is to read or view stories of courageous people. Such stories abound in our faith traditions. The book of Esther from the Hebrew scriptures, and Stephen's brave retort to his captors in the seventh chapter of Acts immediately come to mind. Also, the story of the Prophet Muhammad's refusal to give in to demands to renounce Allah shows his willingness to be put to death for his faith.

War, of course, provides ample opportunity for sacrifice and risk. Michael Shaara's great novel, *The Killer Angels*, is the basis of the film *Gettysburg*, both of which have examples of courage in the face of great loss and tragedy. Another story set during war is *Schindler's List*, though Oskar Schindler's courage occurs not on the battlefield, but behind the scenes.

One can also look to people and events from the civil rights and women's movements for examples of bravery. A great children's book with a bit of suspense and a surprise ending is Robert Coles' *The Story of Ruby Bridges*. My high school students were knocked out by the film *Iron Jawed Angels* about Alice Paul, Lucy Burns and their compatriots who were jailed, beaten, and force-fed for daring to picket the White House for the right to vote.

These are all stories that are entertaining and also serve to prime our minds so we will show courage when the time comes.

Listening Suggestions

Links to audio and video files are found at
www.livelikelouis.com.

"(What Did I Do to Be So) Black and Blue" is from the Broadway show in which Louis became a breakout star in 1929. Originally the tune was written for a black woman considered too black (as opposed to "browns and yellers") to get a man. Louis altered the lyrics to be more generally about the situation of blacks in an officially racist America. He performed it throughout his career.

"Fables of Faubus" is a piece by Charles Mingus of the next generation of jazz musicians, more outspoken and edgy in their approach to race in America. In this piece, without using words the musicians satirize the racist governor, portraying him as a buffoon. Mockery is often the sharpest put-down. See what you think.

In 1970 Louis recorded the anthem of the civil rights movement, "We Shall Overcome." Many stars and friends, including Tony Bennett and jazz pioneer Miles Davis, were on hand to comprise the backing choir. He quieted them before recording the song, urging them to "sing like you never sang before. This is a beautiful song and it's our song."

9   Body and Soul

*in which Louis shows us
the power of purpose*

When you watch the movie "Hello Dolly," you have to wait almost until the end, during the big production number with its chorus of singing waiters. All of a sudden, there's Satchmo in a wonderful cameo appearance, singing that famous title song with Barbara Streisand. His charm and voice are in full force, though he looks drawn. For by 1968, when the movie was shot, fifty years of constant touring had caught up with him. He went in to see the doctor later that year, was diagnosed with congestive heart failure, and was hospitalized. He told his doctor, Gary Zucker, his life "wasn't worth anything" if he couldn't play his trumpet. After rest and medical treatment, he was released in spring of 1969. For the first time in his life, he became a homebody in Queens. He made reel-to-reel recordings of himself reflecting on his life, created collages on the tape boxes, and wrote more memoirs. Sometimes he would walk around the house with his trumpet in his hands, occasionally blowing into it just a bit, against doctor's orders. Performing on it was out of the question, according to the doctor; but any long-term retirement was out of the question, according to Louis Armstrong.

In 1970 he recorded two albums, just singing. It wasn't enough. In the fall of that year he started playing again, calling the All Stars back into existence for a stint in Vegas and making numerous TV appearances including the one with Johnny Cash mentioned earlier. In March of 1971 Pops took a two-week engagement at New York's Waldorf-Astoria hotel. His doctor thought it would kill him, but after talking with Louis, they compromised: Pops could play if he took a room at the hotel and left it only to go downstairs and perform. To Louis Armstrong, music was life, and he completed what would be his last engagement. What had led Dr. Zucker to compromise was Louis's response when informed the two-week gig might kill him: "Doc, that's all right, I don't care. My whole life, my whole soul, my whole spirit is to blooow that horn."

And It Really Was

Louis Armstrong certainly knew what he was about. Though not the stereotypical, grim workaholic, Louis made it clear throughout his life that music was his priority, mainly through his horn. When people with only a passing familiarity with Louis now hear his name, they'll often respond with a comment about his singing, perhaps even imitating it. Certainly, singing was a big part of his appeal. But in his mind he was a trumpet-playing entertainer on a mission to bring happiness to people. He knew what he was about and he stuck to it, thereby living a life of meaning and purpose.

In New York in the 1920s, it bothered him that his band mates spent their off-duty time drinking and playing cards instead of listening to, and learning from, other musicians. As an evening progressed and his colleagues' liquor took its toll, their sloppy demeanor on the bandstand irked him even more. He was a musical athlete surrounded by teammates not nearly as dedicated as he. "When I pick up that horn, that's all. The world's behind me, and I don't concentrate on nothin' but it. . . . That's my livin' and my life."

And though his fourth marriage was a good one, he made plain his priority: "First comes my horn, and then Lucille. But the horn comes first." This wasn't to disparage the woman he loved for three decades. When Louis said this in the 1950s, he had been supporting himself and others by his trumpet playing for nearly forty years; his immense fame had shown him how important his talent was to the world. His New York Times obituary included a quote that summarizes his life's purpose:

I never tried to prove nothing, just always wanted to give a good show. My life has been my music, it's always come first, but the music ain't worth nothing if you can't lay it on the public. The main thing is to live for that audience, 'cause what you're there for is to please the people.

The Power of a Purpose

It's clear that Louis Armstrong felt his life had a purpose. Many people feel the same way. As thinking beings who create objects to serve functions, we naturally want to know what purpose *we* were created for. We want to believe that our be-ing is not just an accident or coincidence, and that surviving and passing on genes is not all there is to the game of life. Psychiatrist and Holocaust survivor Victor Frankl called this "man's search for meaning" in his famous book of the same name.

But many people don't feel a purpose to their lives. Unlike most human beings throughout time, many of us in modern society haven't been taught a Truth accepted by everyone around us. There now is not one, standard version of who the god or gods are, what the world is, what our place in it is, or what proper living is. Since our culture lacks one, unquestioned Truth, it instead presents each of us with a number of religions, philosophies, and worldviews from which to choose. This great variety of ideas, each with its ardent believers, has had the effect of leaving many of us adrift with no over-arching reason for living. Lacking a purpose for existence, it's easy then to live on autopilot, imitating those around us or taking our cues from advertisers and the mass media. Others do sense something is wrong and incomplete; they feel ill at ease, even empty. "Anomie" is what sociologist Emile Durkheim called this feeling, literally "without a guiding principle." You can find this form of anomie sometimes in retirees (usually men) who lived to work and find nothing to take its place when their career ends. Pastor Rick Warren has certainly tapped into our desire for a sense of meaning and mission, selling 30 million copies of his book, *The Purpose-Driven Life*.

Like Pastor Warren, many people do derive a sense of purpose from their religion. Their reason for existing is usually to serve God and/or do good for others. Some people have even more specific purposes: they exist to support their family or to raise their children to be healthy and compassionate people. Still others live for their career, maybe just to move up a corporate ladder, or to make the world better through a service or product. As behavioral scientists have studied happiness in the last decade or so, they've found one of the key ingredients is this sense of mission, especially being in service to a cause greater than oneself. Lecturer Tal Ben-Shahar taught Harvard's most popular class, Positive Psychology, and he writes, "Happiness lies at the intersection between pleasure and meaning. Whether at work or at home, the goal is to engage in activities that are both personally significant and enjoyable." Researcher Ed Diener has found that "as humans we actually require a sense of meaning to thrive."

One way to feel a sense of purpose and meaning is to consciously state it and keep it in mind. A helpful tool is a personal mission or purpose statement. Now, I know if you were in the business world in the 1990s, the odds are at least fifty-fifty you served (or were forced to serve) on a committee to write a corporate mission statement. It's easy to mock many that were produced that way. Being a sucker for things that sound as if they'll do some good, I helped craft a mission statement both at work and at church. The one at work was typical of the bad ones: too wordy and promptly forgotten. It's too bad, because if people know and believe in an organization's mission, it can certainly help them and the company. Too often, though, the statements were corporate gobbledy-gook, which Scott Adams' *Dilbert* website ably mocked with an online mission statement generator. It cobbled together random words and phrases that unfortunately ended up sounding remarkably like many actual corporate statements: "The purpose of SatchCo is to dynamically interface with multiple vendor inputs, while maximizing integral buy-in, to deliver the most cost-integrated service possible to our end users." Look online and you'll find websites with real-life examples just as incomprehensible, foisted on employees who deserved better.

But a good mission statement – now that really can be beneficial, helping to keep the main thing the main thing. My church's purpose statement was concise and memorable. We used it on bulletins and signs and spoke of it in meetings and worship. Our purpose was to love God and other people, and to help people become followers of Jesus. Maybe some activities would stray from the stated purpose of the group, but at least they could be evaluated in light of our mission, to see if they should continue. The U.S. Army's purpose statement is very concise and gives clear direction to the group. The army exists "to fight and win our nation's wars." I have a personal purpose statement for my career, which I use in my email signature: to help young people gain knowledge and become better thinkers. I'm far from perfect at this, but the words guide me to choose what I have the kids do in class and at home.

Even without an overt mission statement, some people are still very purpose-driven, committed to something larger than just subsisting and buying whatever new things gets marketed at them. Some of the most focused people I know of don't usually have a written statement, but they nevertheless feel an intensely strong sense of purpose: Olympic athletes. Their mission is to place as high as they can in the medal competition, ideally to be standing on the top platform hearing their national anthem ringing out. This purpose guides how they spend nearly every minute of every day, down to every morsel of food and drop of liquid they put in their bodies. Whether it's an image of being on the medal stand, defeating an enemy, or producing better thinkers, having a purpose guides behavior and makes success more likely in any endeavor. As we learned in this book's introduction, beginning with the end in mind is one of Steven Covey's famous seven habits of highly effective people.

A sense of mission can also help you prepare for the future. Although a person might stumble into success occasionally, your chances rise dramatically the better prepared you are. The Allied leaders knew in 1944 their mission was to successfully land a sizable invasion force in France. This clear and simple purpose, closely connected with the larger goal of defeating Germany, guided them in all their months of planning and rehearsing for D-Day. Likewise I've seen a strong sense of purpose (often to become a doctor or dentist) motivate students to study hard for years and years ahead of time. So often, the success we see is the result of considerable hard work done outside of the limelight, all motivated by having a mission in mind.

Louis's sense of purpose led him to live it out through his work. I almost hesitate to call it "work," since that word has the connotation of being unenjoyable or even distasteful, something you *have* to do. True, he earned his living from music, but performing was obviously a joy to Louis. "Do what you love and you'll never work a day in your life," the saying goes. Writer Joseph Campbell advised us to "follow our bliss," and so Satchmo did. Following that bliss and earning his living were one and the same. "Pops loved to play the horn," one of his sidemen observed. "That's what kept him going. If we had two or three days off, he'd get restless and was ready to play again."

Some people assumed longtime manager Joe Glaser was a slave-driver, forcing Louis to play an endless string of one-nighters. Actually, the reverse was true. Louis's friend, cornetist Ruby Braff, recalled the manager actually wanting to carve some time out of his client's performing schedule for other projects. Louis reportedly told Glaser, "You ever give me a night off, go find yourself a new boy." Braff recalled, "Every night was a party for him. For him to have four weeks of no parties was like, 'What are you doing me, a big favor?'" Once,

Louis was somehow convinced to take an eight-week vacation cruise. Rather than lay off the band, Louis's management gave them a paid vacation. Clarinetist Joe Darensbourg recalled just getting into the swing of relaxing beside the swimming pool when the phone rang. The office was calling to cut short his leisure. Louis had gotten bored on the cruise and needed to get back to work playing his trumpet, bringing happiness to his hearers.

Recall how, even when his health was failing him, Louis kept performing, first vocally, then again on trumpet. He kept on doing what he felt he was meant to do, what he *had* to do. So, his life continued to be meaningful. Researchers have shown that continuing to do the things that give us pleasure and meaning reduces stress and lessens depression. Given the precarious state of his health in the early 1970s, his return to performing and living out his purpose probably kept Louis living longer than he would have, in a forced retirement.

Serving a Purpose in a Less-Than-Ideal Job

For any number of reasons, you might not feel "called" to the job you have. You might not even like it, much less love it, as Louis loved playing music. I'm not going to glibly tell you to just change careers, and start doing what you most enjoy. In an ideal world, yes, that would be most preferable. But I'm enough of a realist to know that, for some very important reasons, a career change might not be possible or the best choice. Children need feeding and mortgages need paying. If I felt I had been meant all along to be a professional jazz musician and quit teaching, with its good salary and health benefits, that would certainly be an unloving act toward my family, who depend on me.

If you're a student, however – because of your position near life's starting gate – you likely *are* in a position to discern an occupational calling and answer it. It's not always possible (due to those pesky food and rent bills), but often it is. I highly recommend the bestselling career-choice and self-discovery book, *What Color Is Your Parachute?* There's a good chance you'll get a copy for graduation. Yes, the Dr. Seuss book about the places you'll go has a snazzier cover (and Seuss-ian rhyming), but *Parachute* is really worth reading and doing the activities it provides.

For those seemingly stuck – at least for the time being – in a job you don't love, you still have some options. You can regularly, deliberately think of your job's good qualities. Try doing this during the morning commute, rather than anticipating things that might go wrong as we're so prone to do. What we think about earlier affects how we perceive and respond later. Also, you can give thanks for those positives as you remember them. One of the secrets to happiness is wanting what you have, and giving thanks helps that feeling arise. Furthermore, you can find or develop a mission within your work role. Someone who feels stuck as, say, a landscape worker, could envision a mission to create beauty or bring order out of chaos.

If there is a specific calling you feel, a bliss you

would follow, you can often pursue it as an amateur (Latin for someone who does something "for
the love of it"). If I felt that calling to be a musician,
but needed to remain a teacher to support my family, I could play jazz on the side. I would occasionally make some dough, and might also volunteer
for the local arts center's benefits or play in church
or temple. Since doing anything for your living can
become a drag, this might in fact be a more blissful
way of following it, rather than making music my
day job.

Regardless of how you come to it, sensing a
purpose, feeling yourself to be on a mission, is the
antidote to the zombie-esque life of quiet despera-
tion Thoreau saw most people leading. Knowing
and fulfilling a mission at home or work can transform it from drudgery or a necessary evil, into a
venue in which to fulfill a purpose and find meaning. Of course you will sometimes wander or become distracted from it; welcome to the human
race. But knowing your purpose will inspire you as
Louis's did him. It will imbue your thoughts and
actions with meaning and power.

Practices

One Specific Calling?

As far as a general purpose for your existence, we'll save that for the final chapter. Let's focus for now on more specific purposes. Louis felt a very specific calling, a "first thing" he kept first all his life: playing the trumpet for people to enjoy. Similarly, some of us live our lives with one specific purpose whether we are aware of it or not. Some live almost exclusively for their children. Others live to achieve higher standing in a community or corporation. Still others live for their job or profession. It's good to acknowledge such a purpose, whether just to make it overt and affirm it, or to examine its worth. See if you can finish the sentence below.

My actions show I live specifically to _____.

If you don't perceive one, specific purpose or mission to your life, rest easy, neither do I. I have many interests and activities. If you do perceive one – especially if you hadn't realized it before – give thought to that purpose and how it can be used for good. Likely it's worthy, but occasionally we can look back and see what we were living for was misguided. Self-examination is never wasted.

Having a Purpose for Each Role

If you (like me) don't feel one, dominant calling like playing the trumpet or being a dental assistant, you still play certain roles in life. Developing and feeling a purpose in these roles will help guide you to perform them more happily and successfully. I mentioned a purpose I have in my teaching. In another area of life, as a father, my purpose is to produce adults who are as capable as they can be, and who contribute positively to other people. Try writing some sentences like the following, for each of your different roles or settings:

As a(n)_____,
my purpose is to _____.

At _____,
my purpose is to _____.

I have my teaching mission posted in two places in my classroom. You might use the ol' sticky-note trick to keep each role's purpose before you. Remembering these purposes will guide your actions so you will keep the main thing the main thing and be more successful.

Listening Suggestions

Links to audio and video files are found at
www.livelikelouis.com.

With these tunes, we'll bookend Pops' career. "Just Gone" is the earliest recording of Louis Armstrong. You'll have to listen hard to hear him. He plays the second (lower) cornet part with King Oliver's group in 1923. The story goes that in these early recordings, the studio was very narrow and Louis had to be placed far in the back, his playing was so strong.

At the far end of Louis's life is "Whistle While You Work," from his album of Disney tunes. This is from the last recording session of the last album to feature Pops on trumpet. Plus, it's about enjoying your work, which Louis did with gusto for over fifty years.

An attitude of joy: Pops at work, sharing happiness with his audience at Carnegie Hall, February 1947.

10 What a Wonderful World

*in which Louis reminds us
of our ultimate purpose*

We've encountered Louis in the recording studio several times already. First we saw him dropping some lyrics but going with the flow by scat singing. Then, nearly forty years later, we witnessed him recording an obscure show tune that became a monster hit. "Hello Dolly" was so huge, in fact, Pops then made a number of similar recordings of Broadway songs done his way. Now we meet him in 1967 about to record a song that will wonderfully deviate from that formula.

Sometimes we look back on the sixties through little, round, rose-colored glasses. Before studying the period, my students often picture a carefree time of sun-dappled hippies dancing in a park, arms upraised and eyes blissfully shut. Certainly there was a spirit of opportunity and positive change in the air. Just as certainly, though, there was strife and hatred: shocking assassinations, riots, vitriolic resistance to the civil rights movement, and the endless jungle warfare that was Vietnam.

Record producer Bob Thiele set out to write a song to counter all the bad nightly news. He wanted to emphasize "the love and sharing people make possible for themselves and each other every day." His song, "What a Wonderful World," spoke of simple things: trees, clouds, babies, growth. It spoke of the natural rhythm of day and night, and of the bond of brotherly love among friends. Since he had earlier produced an album for Louis, Thiele knew his song matched well with the entertainer's outlook on life and that he was just the right person to sing it. He made a demonstration record of the tune and visited Louis on the road. While the demo was still playing, Louis interrupted with the name he used for all his friends: "Pops, I dig it. Let's do it."

Louis had no long-term contract with any record label, so they went to Thiele's label, ABC-Paramount Records. Because of the extra cost to hire an orchestra, Louis accepted the minimum pay allowed by the musicians' union, only about $250. The head of the label, Larry Newton, sat in the control room. But he couldn't abide the fact that his label wasn't recording another up-tempo Satchmo romp like "Dolly." As the session went on, he became more and more upset. Why abandon a formula that worked, and was liable to make more (possibly much more) money than this sappy ballad? Newton got madder and madder at what he saw as a missed opportunity for profit. He reached a breaking point and proclaimed the session over. He would send all the musicians home and scrap the whole thing, basically "firing" the legendary

Louis Armstrong. Thiele, much to his credit, coura-
geously ordered the company president out of the
control room. As we know, the record was finished,
the world responded to its message of hope, and it
became a big, wonderful hit.

In England. There the record was number one
with a bullet, as Casey Kasem used to say, selling
over half a million copies. But not in America. Newton wouldn't allow his company to promote the record. Louis performed it on the *The Tonight Show*
and in concert, but the recording remained essentially unknown in the States until 1987. The song
finally found its deserved fame in America through
its use in the film *Good Morning, Vietnam*. The song
plays ironically underneath scenes of bombing and
destruction, some of the strife Thiele wanted to
counter. Still, the positive song struck a chord with
Americans. Two decades after its initial release,
"Wonderful World" was re-issued as a single,
earned a spot in the Top 40, and was eventually selected for the Grammy Hall of Fame in 1999. Now
any Armstrong compilation CD is incomplete without it. Rather than being best known for a (very
fine) ditty about a Dolly, Louis is most remembered
for a song about friendship, love, and appreciating
the simple things of life.

Although jazz critics might prefer Louis to be
best known for one of his trumpet masterpieces,
could there be any song that better matches the
man? While researching this book, I was struck by
the positivity of Louis's language, how often he fla-
vored his speech and writing with words like
"beautiful," "wonderful," and "lovely." When

Louis introduced older tunes, he felt compelled to praise them twice in one sentence, announcing, "Now for one of those good ol' good ones . . ." We've seen earlier how he saw beyond the flaws of lesser musicians, focusing on the good they had to offer. And when he remembered his upbringing in New Orleans among poverty and crime, he would often speak of it in kind or even humorous terms, accentuating the positive. As legendary record producer George Avakian remarked, Satchmo's ever-present smile was no act, but "a smile that came from within, all the way. He took everything that came his way and he turned it into an asset no matter what happened to him."

Two thousand years ago, my favorite rabbi put it this way: "The eye is the lamp for the body; if your eye be healthy, your whole body will be full of light." In other words, the more positively we see the world, the more positive world we'll be living in. One day, for example, I listened to a positive speaker urge me (via an ancient technology known as "cassette") to say to myself, "Something good is gonna happen to me today." Throughout the day I had taken her advice and repeated those words. That night, I was reading near a window. I noticed a very bright light coming from over my shoulder. I turned and looked outside. No, not an angel! It was the moon shining very brightly. Now, on a normal night I would've just turned back around (or even grumped about the glare); but that night, thanks to the earlier priming of my mind, I noticed how beautiful the moon was. A good thing happened to me simply because I had the eyes to see it as good.

Viewing things as positive is the quickest way to have more positive things happen to you.

Someone else with Louis's upbringing and the grueling decades he spent on the road might have looked back bitterly. But because of his outlook, for Louis those same circumstances could prompt him to remark near the end, "I think I've had a beautiful life." And so he did. Because Louis saw good, he thus was full of light and able to share it back to the world. Looking back, Pops wrote, "My whole life has been happiness. Through all of the misfortunes, etc., I did not plan anything. Life was there for me and I accepted it. And life, whatever came out, has been beautiful to me, and I love everybody."

Our Great Purpose

Let us return to Larry Newton, the executive who wanted to stop the recording session. Please remember, as Pops would, that he had some good qualities. We know this because he was a human being and we all have some. I'm sorry the story presents him as kind of a villain. After all, his job was to maximize shareholder value. Yet, you can't help but see a contrast between Newton, concerned about money and wanting to see a record fail; and Louis, wanting to get out of a rut and give people a song of hope and joy. Through this contrast we see Louis's larger purpose, which he lived throughout his life. We spoke last chapter of Louis's living to play his trumpet. He spoke of that purpose many times, as we've seen. But in a comment he made about his audiences, you can hear that even the horn was a means to a larger end: "People love me and my music and you know I love them. The minute I walk on the bandstand, they know they're going to get something good. I see to that."

All through his life, through his music and through his person, Louis lived to contribute to the good of others.

This is not to say he was perfect. Like Larry Newton and you and me, being human he was also flawed. Nevertheless, with his music he brought joy to millions. In his personal life, he deliberately treated people with kindness and generosity. Throughout his life, starting as a boy supporting his family, to old age, checking with neighborhood kids about their homework, Louis was a *contributor*.

Maybe this seems an odd or cold word to describe the outgoing Louis Armstrong. I used to dislike the word, myself, when people would speak of wanting to raise children to become "contributing members of society." It seemed bland, like producing unthinking cogs for the machine. But upon reflection, a "contributor" implies activity, as opposed to a passive cog just spinning in place. A contributor adds to the well-being and well-functioning of another person, a family, a community, an organization. A contributor applies thought, word, and deed toward some good end: easing pain, encouraging joy, helping someone grow. Now I think being a contributor is *precisely* what I want for my own children, according to their different talents and personalities.

We noted in an earlier chapter how it's natural

to focus on negatives. However, it's also natural to cooperate and contribute. As social animals we inherit the urge to help others. In our pre-history, individuals who helped those they lived with raise their kids, hunt food, or defend the cave, would be helped in turn by those same comrades, thus passing on genes for an inclination to cooperate. "Together Everyone Achieves More," the sports adage goes. This survival advantage to helping others is probably why we get that reward of a warm feeling when we help someone in need, and why spending twenty dollars on another person "leads to greater boosts in happiness than spending that money on oneself." True, we're hardwired to compete and care about ourselves, but we're also hardwired to care about and contribute to the good of other people. Caring for others is so common – and having truly no empathy is so rare – we even have labels for people who are purely selfish: "psychopaths" or "sociopaths."

Caring for others and seeking their good is bred deep in the bone, etched into our being long before we were even *Homo sapiens*. In an experiment in 1964, researchers found that rhesus monkeys would refuse to pull a chain that gave them food when it also gave a shocking jolt of electricity to a fellow monkey. One went almost two weeks without food, to keep another from feeling pain. Famed primatologist Frans de Waal remarks, "Those primates were literally starving themselves" to help others. Numerous observations and studies have shown how chimps, our nearest relatives, live and work together, kiss to make up, even console each other after a loss by putting an arm around the other's shoulder.

In addition to a biological urge to do good, many religions teach that being oriented toward our fellow human beings is also morally right. The Hebrew scriptures include many provisions for participating positively in the lives of others, from shared rituals to leaving the edges of farm fields unharvested, so the poor and foreigners might "glean" some food for themselves. The book of Leviticus instructs its readers to "love your neighbor as yourself," later quoted by Jesus of Nazareth when asked to name the greatest commandment of all. Of course much of his teaching, and the rest of the New Testament, exhorts his followers to live lovingly by helping others and participating in the shared life known as "the body of Christ." Charitable giving is so important to Islam it is one of its five pillars. Other religions, too, teach that we should live out a love for God by caring for other people and contributing to the greater good. The Dalai Lama says, "My religion is very simple. My religion is kindness."

For those of us in the fast-growing classification "spiritual but not religious," we can deduce this grand purpose to life not from a religious book or teachings, but from the unfolding story of the universe. It is a story of small, simple wholes that, over time, come together, collaborate, and cooperate into larger wholes. *These* wholes, in turn, combine with similar units into another, more complex whole with its own emergent properties. Which then cooperates with others into a new, larger thing, and so on, and so on: energy to matter to subatomics to atoms to molecules to substances to cells to tissues to organs to organisms to communities to societies to . . . ?

Some thinkers even describe the universe itself as being conscious now. That sounds pretty "out there." But we say that "you" are conscious, even though only part of you really performs that function. So the cosmos itself can likewise be considered conscious, since *it* has a thinking part (us). Moreover, just as the cells and organs in your body combine and cooperate to produce a healthy you, so individual humans all over the planet have been combining and collaborating in fits and starts for thousands of years to become healthy families, communities, and societies. Now many of us are participating, especially through trade and the internet, in a new, emerging whole. A species in which a large number of members truly combine their thoughts and cultures is a new thing, a social organism made up of individual human beings, but having properties all its own. And through reason, creativity, and free will, we can influence how We/It develops. The eminent futurist Barbara Marx Hubbard calls this "conscious evolution."

Thus we can deliberately take our place in this ongoing development, contributing and collaborating, helping others who in turn will add to the emerging Us. Is this morally imperative? Stephen Tramel, a wonderful philosophy professor, warned us that you can't get an "ought" from an "is." That is, just because the universe is a great chain of ever-developing collaboration, it's a bad leap of logic to say people *ought* – are morally obligated – to live likewise. Nevertheless, cooperating and contributing is living in right relationship with the *Logos*, the underlying order and creative principle of the cosmos. To this observer (and many others) it just seems right to live in harmony with the ongoing direction of the universe.

So, you can arrive at positive, proactive living as the purpose for your existence from either of two starting points. From the pathway of traditional religion, it's a response to God, to whom you're grateful, and who desires this of you. It is healthy, whole living as God has designed for you. Coming from a scientific, evolutionary understanding, a life based on contributing and collaborating is in accord with the progression of all things, singing in tune with the Music of the Spheres, a composition in development for fourteen billion years and counting. The good news is, regardless of your starting point, this way lies true and meaningful life.

How Louis Contributed

Louis lived life for the benefit of others. Foremost was the joy he gave back through his glorious trumpeting and soulful singing. His comments from that period describe the higher purpose he and his music achieved with his audiences.

> They get their soul lifted because they got
> the same soul I have the minute I hit a note.
> . . . I love my audience and they love me and

we just have one good time whenever I get
up on the stage – it's such a lovely pleasure.

People responded to Louis's gift of happiness with
such enthusiasm all over the world, he was nick-
named "Ambassador Satch" in the 1950s. To borrow from Jesus's words again, Louis not only returned to the world the light his healthy eyes saw,
he received it back again in good measure, pressed
down, shaken together, and running over.

Louis Armstrong found his niche in the great
endeavor of adding to the good. His was to use music to share love and joy with his hearers; he even
described himself as being "in the service of happiness." But as important as happiness is, it's only one
way to build up or bless others. Another person,
quiet and good at numbers, will find a different
way to contribute. A serious person who likes making things in wood will find yet another. A boisterous soul in the business world, still another.

Betty Erni finds her place to contribute in the
pressbox elevator of Ford Field, home of the Detroit
Lions. Columnist Michael Rosenberg calls this elevator operator "the most openly happy person I
have ever met." In her elevator Betty is uncon-
cerned that she's unable to watch the game on Sun-
days (perhaps part of the secret of her happiness).
"I'm too busy thinking: Who is going to get on my
elevator that I can bless?" Whatever your personality and talents, you too have family members, co-
workers, neighbors, and strangers you interact
with: people who get on your elevator, so to speak,
all of whom you can intend well-being toward, and

try to bless. The important thing is to be about the work of contributing however you're able.

Louis spread love in many avenues of life. He adopted his cousin's son when he himself was just a teen. He was very generous, giving away thousands of dollars a year in cash, "greasing the mitts" of people who came to his dressing room, and sending monthly envelopes to old friends in need. In his old age Louis and Lucille would invite the neighborhood kids in to watch TV and have ice cream. His overall positive demeanor uplifted those around him; he was one of those people who make you feel better just by entering a room. George Avakian said, "He was the finest person that I ever knew among all the artists I worked with. I mean that as a human being. He was a terrific guy, just as genuine as can be, and he was a gentleman in every respect, treated people very, very well. He was a – he's just one of the finest people I ever met in my life."

Louis knew the great purpose of blessing and contributing. Maybe it was in his DNA to see the good and be positive. Or, maybe he absorbed it by watching the way his mother or granny acted. Maybe both. And maybe you've known a few such people like Louis, folks for whom very positive thinking and living seem to be as easy as breathing.

To others of us (including your author), positivity doesn't come so naturally. We often find ourselves eating, breathing, working, and recreating without much thought about it or, worse, focusing on the negatives. We who are like that need to keep our Great Purpose more consciously in mind. We need to be reminded of our higher calling so we'll find ways to live it out, even if that just means viewing what we're already doing through the lens of contributing to others.

Fortunately, there are people to help us be mindful of our common calling to contribute and build others up. That's the purpose of this chapter, and of entire books by inspiring authors far more skilled than I. There are websites and daily email services built to remind us of life's deeper truth. And, as noted above, living for others is a focus of all the great faiths, which have preachers, teachers, musicians, and writers to inspire us. Last and not least are the ordinary people who, in their approach to life, are actually extra-ordinary: the friends, co-workers, and associates close at hand who are especially loving and positive, people we can be with and emulate.

The subtitle of this book makes an implied promise that living like Louis will help you lead a better life. Truth be told, the point of living isn't just to have yourself a wonderful life. It's to help create a more wonderful world. Late in Louis's life, in the midst of personally answering hundreds of fan letters, his secretary asked how he handled all the love sent his way. Louis admitted it could occasionally get heavy. In five words, though, he summarized his approach to life and his response to people's outpouring of love:

"I give it right back."

Let us go and do likewise.

Practices

Eye Care

We heard earlier that a healthy eye sees the good and fills your whole body with light. More concretely, as we see good and intend good, we actually influence other people to act more positively. This is thanks to some brain cells we all have called mirror neurons. You've experienced this many times, often without even knowing. If someone seems nervous, you'll probably get a bit nervous too, and respond guardedly. If someone seems aggressive, right away you will be too, at least a little bit. On the other hand, if you approach someone openly and positively, he or she will usually mirror that and be more prone to treat you well in return, creating a positive feedback loop.

But what if you're not naturally positive? As we noted in chapter six, there's a strong survival instinct to attend to negatives and want to fix them. How can you come to look on things more positively? This is the focus of many books including Martin Seligman's bestseller, *Learned Optimism*. It's also a common focus of cognitive therapy, which involves having people identify where their thinking is unhelpful, then learning and practicing new scripts to say internally when reacting or reflecting.

Like many worthwhile endeavors (including the road to Carnegie Hall), common to all approaches is practice. Here are a few specifics to try:

List your blessings in writing every morning, or some other regular time. Maybe in the business world, lunch time would be especially helpful, to re-set your mind after a stressful morning. Remember to name things whose goodness is because of their absence, for instance, "I don't have a cold anymore."

You can also list some people or things you often feel negative toward and try to write something positive about them. Again, this is not to deny that sometimes there are certainly problems that need dealing with. However, viewing a challenge differently might help you engage it more proactively.

Many people speak or write out affirmations daily. Try the site *Vital Affirmations* (found at www.vitalaffirmations.com) for some good ones to recite. My favorite? "Life is a joy filled with delightful surprises."

Finally, praying daily for others – aside from the good it might do them directly – certainly will help you be more care-full toward them and toward people in general.

Remembering Your Great Purpose

Years ago I was given the high honor of addressing three hundred graduating high school students at their commencement ceremony. Rather than tell them what to do, I shared and elaborated on a phrase I had recently heard, the Truth I hope you sensed at the heart of this final chapter:

True living comes only through giving.

Of course, "giving" here means more than money, though our materialistic culture has trained us to think of that immediately. There is a famous trinity of T's involved in giving: time, talent, and, yes, treasure. This holistic understanding of giving is just another way of saying what we've called "contributing": putting energy into helping, healing, and building up. As the phrase often attributed to Winston Churchill goes, "We make a living by what we get. We make a life by what we give." Although he didn't actually say that, what he did say is just as inspiring:

> What is the use of living, if it be not to strive for noble causes and to make this muddled world a better place for those who will live in it after we are gone? How else can we put ourselves in harmonious relation with the great verities and consolations of the infinite and the eternal?

To keep this high calling in mind, one way is to associate with others who do. If not in person, you can commune with such people through reading and listening to their words.

Another way to remember our great purpose is by deliberately calling it to mind on a regular basis. In chapter four I offered a simple guided relaxation technique involving simple thoughts coordinated with breathing. As a means of remembering and putting into practice our great mission, here's another one, focusing on the truth of giving and living. As before, sit comfortably in a quiet room. Notice your breathing. Let your mind be as relaxed as you can. Do nothing for about three breaths.

After that, each time you inhale, think,
"True living . . ."

As you exhale, think,
". . . comes only through giving."

Breathe at whatever tempo feels natural; your body will do what's right for you. Continue this for a minute. Repeat as needed. Again, when your mind wanders, gently bring it back to focus on the task at hand with no self-reproach. Feel free to increase the duration if you continue on with this type of meditation, what Christianity calls "breath prayer."

Let me admit here at the end of our last section on practices that I am a pretty normal American: I often forget or neglect to do what's good for me. In fact, as I write this there is a neglected bottle of men's vitamins calling to me from the back of the cupboard. Old habits and the tyranny of the urgent die hard. But when I do remember to practice what has been offered in these sections, I feel better and am a better person. I believe the same will be true for you.

Be well.

Listening Suggestions

Links to audio and video files are found at
www.livelikelouis.com.

Pops was the first jazz musician to record "When
the Saints Go Marchin' In." He performed the joyful, rollicking tune countless times with the All
Stars. The phrase, "Oh how I want to be in that
number," originally referred to the number of people ("saints") who would be allowed to march into
heaven. The New Testament Greek word for "saint"
is *hagios*, meaning "set aside for a special purpose."
In this way, we can think of saints not in a "holier-
than-thou" way, but as people meant for the very
important purpose of contributing to the good and
building others up. Oh, how I want to be in that
number. I bet you do too.

   In 1970 some of Pops' friends put some new lyrics to the old tune, and re-titled it "Boy From New
Orleans." In this version, Louis sings you through
his whole life's story. Near the end, the music
slows, and Pops offers a very touching, spoken
verse that summarizes his lifelong positive outlook
and gratitude. I'll leave it unprinted here, since it
would have about ten percent of the impact it will
have when you hear him say it to you. Historian
Ricky Riccardi has pointed out that Pops closed his
last shows with this tune, so these words of thanks
would have been the last words ever spoken by

Louis onstage. A consummate entertainer and one of humanity's great souls, the boy from New Orleans exited perfectly on a high note of love.

Coda

in which we part, with Louis's blessing

Coda means "tail," and in music the coda is the ending of the piece, when you can tell the musicians are wrapping things up. For instance on "Hello, Dolly," it's when Pops sings, "Dolly – never go away" three times and the musicians finish it off together. So now, O reader, we're at the coda of our exploration of stories from the life of Louis Armstrong. Certainly he had his flaws too, but I've left those to the several thorough biographies you'll find listed in the reading suggestions at the back of this book. This was not to hide anything, but to keep to my double purpose: to encourage and inspire. Any success in those endeavors is due to the terrific person I had the privilege of sharing with you.

We began at the end, with Louis's accomplishments and fame as a way to see how far he traveled. We saw that he transcended a poor, crime-ridden neighborhood and broken family, not letting his circumstances define him. We met two important figures from early in Louis's career, whose encouragement was instrumental in his becoming the musician and person he was. We learned of his being open to different types of people and music, and being able to roll with unexpected changes. We were reminded to enjoy our talents and focus on our strengths, just as Louis was utterly confident of the high C's he kept in his pocket. We heard the story of Lucille surprising Pops with a home, and how much he treasured it and his neighborhood in Queens. Louis's odd devotion to an intense laxative reminded us to indulge our own idiosyncrasies, not being afraid to be ourselves. We heard Louis's stern rebukes against injustice, words that put his rewarding career in jeopardy.

Finally, we learned that Louis knew his life's purpose was to share happiness by playing the trumpet; and how this was part of an overall life of sharing joy and contributing to others' well-being. From a spoken introduction to a version of "What a Wonderful World" recorded the year before his death, Louis Armstrong gives us this benediction:

> *And all I'm saying is*
> *see what a wonderful world it would be*
> *if only we'd give it a chance.*
> *Love, baby, love.*
> *That's the secret . . . yeeaah.*

Acknowledgements

I am very grateful to the following people:

My wife, Jane, for her love, encouragement, forbearance, and proofreading skills.

My editor, Tammy Wiles, for her validation, and skill in perceiving many things I could not.

My father, Gerald R. Lynch, for his encouragement and example of work.

My high school band teacher, Grant Hoemke, who taught us you get out of something as much as you put in; and sparked my love of jazz.

Author and archivist Ricky Riccardi, for his encouragement and help.

Author Jen Brady, for her publishing advice.

Jay Brodersen of Archtop Productions, for his encouragement and example of attempting and completing a large undertaking.

Lauren Beversluis, Lynn Thomas, and Peggy Schumann, for their early enthusiasm.

Michael Shulman of Magnum Photos, for facilitating the use of the cover photo.

Author and radio host John St. Augustine, for inspiring me and giving advice.

Authors Dan Schawbel and Roger C. Parker, for unknowingly prompting me to write a book.

The staff of Book World, for market research.

Many friends and colleagues, for encouragement and feedback online.

Suggestions for Further Reading

For a thorough exploration of Louis's life, either of these biographies is a great place to start:

Giddins, Gary. *Satchmo: The Genius of Louis Armstrong.* Boston: Da Capo Press, 2001.

This is a terrific, short bio by Gary Giddins, perhaps our finest living jazz writer. The 2001 paperback is fine, but if you can get your hands on the large-format 1988 version (New York: Doubleday), it's full of rare pictures. It was the companion volume to Giddins' award-winning documentary, Satchmo, *available on DVD.*

Teachout, Terry. *Pops.* Boston: Houghton Mifflin Harcourt, 2009.

Of the longer biographies, this is the one to read, though Bergreen's (see notes) is also good. Teachout, drama critic for the Wall Street Journal, *is an excellent writer and explores Louis's life completely and sympathetically.*

If you wish to go deeper, try any of these:

Armstrong, Louis. *Louis Armstrong in His Own Words.* Edited by Thomas Brothers. Oxford: Oxford University Press, 1999.

_____. *Satchmo: My Life in New Orleans*. New York: Prentice-Hall, 1954.

Brothers has done yeoman's work assembling a very interesting collection of essays and memoirs — some previously unpublished — written by the Man himself. Pops could write. You'll really get a feel for New Orleans in the early 1900s from Louis's vivid memoirs.

Brower, Stephen. *Satchmo: The Wonderful World and Art of Louis Armstrong*. New York: Abrams, 2009.

Brower has produced a beautiful coffee-table book of Louis's tape-box collages and photos.

Riccardi, Ricky. *The Wonderful World of Louis Armstrong* (website), http://dippermouth.blogspot.com

_____. *What a Wonderful World: The Magic of Louis Armstrong's Later Years*. New York: Pantheon, 2011.

Riccardi is a jazz historian with an encyclopedic knowledge of all things Pops. It's an understatement to call his website a blog: each entry is article-length, usually focusing on a particular song or recording session, with copious info about various versions and takes. Entries include embedded audio and/or video too. His book is exactly what the subtitle promises: with many interesting anecdotes and details, Ric-

cardi thoroughly chronicles Louis's last twenty-five years. He gracefully refutes the too-widely-held notion that Pops had nothing new to offer after 1950.

Notes & Photo Credits

*Below are citations of specific sources. Information or
quotations widely available are not cited.*

Epigraph

Bach said: Richard Brookhiser, *Right Time, Right Place: Coming of
Age with William F. Buckley Jr. and the Conservative Movement* (New York: Basic Books, 2009), 174.

Intro

"Armstrong is to music": "Louis Armstrong Quotes and Trib-
utes," *Satchmo.com*, http://www.satchmo.com/
louisarmstrong/quotes.html (accessed September 2009).

"America's Bach": Gary Giddins, *Satchmo: the Genius of Louis
Armstrong* (Boston: Da Capo Press, 2001), xiii.

"The bottom line": Reinhold Wagnleitner, ed., *Satchmo Meets
Amadeus* (Innsbruck: StudienVerlag, 2007), 30.

"Armstrong practically invented": Andrew Dansby, "Heading
Towards Centennial, Louis Armstrong Stands Tall," *Rolling Stone*, August 23, 2000.

"Armstrong influenced Billie Holiday": Jerry Tallmer, "Profile:
Tony Bennett," *Thrive NYC*, October 2005, http://www
.nycplus.com/nycp6/tonybennett.html (accessed July
2012).

"Do you realize": Giddins, *Satchmo*, xii.

"Without him, no me": Geoffrey C. Ward and Ken Burns, *Jazz:
An Illustrated History* (New York: Alfred A. Knopf, 2000),
451.

"You can't play anything": "Louis Armstrong Quotes and Trib-
utes."

1 Don't Fence Me In

Details of Louis's departure are found in Louis Armstrong,
  Satchmo: My Life in New Orleans (New York: Prentice-Hall,
  1954; repr., Boston: Da Capo Press, 1986), chap. 1.
Poor but "clean": Laurence Bergreen, *Louis Armstrong: An Ex-
  travagant Life* (New York: Broadway Books, 1997), 84.
All types treated: Armstrong, *Satchmo*, 8-9.
On Saturday mornings: Richard Merryman, "An Interview with
  Louis Armstrong," *Life*, April 15, 1960, 102.
Some fascinating research: Jay Dixit, "Logos: Branded for Life,"
  Psychology Today, June 2008, 28.
"I never did want": Ward and Burns, *Jazz*, 124.
"noble human behavior": Wayne Shorter, preface to Michelle
  Mercer, *Footprints: The Life and Work of Wayne Shorter* (New
  York: Tarcher/Penguin, 2004), xii.
"Every situation": Deepak Chopra, *Twitter* post, https://twitter
  .com/deepakchopra, September 17, 2009, 10:34 a.m.
"Every time": Bergreen, *An Extravagant Life*, 6.

2 Keep the Rhythm Going

Details of Louis Armstrong's time at the Colored Waif's Home
  are found in Louis Armstrong, *Satchmo: My Life in New Or-
  leans*, chap. 3.
"Go get him": Ibid., 34.
"feel good inside; Gee, what a feeling": Ibid., 40.
"Mr. Davis nodded": Ibid., 42.
"I was in": Ibid., 46.
"Louis, I am going": Ibid.
"The way I see it": Louis Armstrong, "Joe Oliver Is Still King," in
  Louis Armstrong in His Own Words, ed. Thomas Brothers
  (Oxford: Oxford University Press, 1999), 38.
"When he played; had a heart": Louis Armstrong, "Scanning the
  History of Jazz," in *Louis Armstrong in His Own Words*, 174.
"guarded with his life": Armstrong, *Satchmo*, 100.
"I shall never forget": Louis Armstrong, "The Goffin Notebooks,"
  in *Louis Armstrong in His Own Words*, 85.
The dueling bandwagons story is found in Armstrong, *Satchmo*,
  98-99.
"I could go into; I had made up": Ibid., 226.

Details of Louis's departure from New Orleans and reception in Chicago are found in Armstrong, *Satchmo,* chap. 14.

"I can never stop loving": Ibid., 100-101.

"Encouragement is the most": Linda Albert, *Cooperative Discipline* (Circle Pines, MN: American Guidance Service, 1996), 15.

A team of sports science researchers: Joseph L. Andreacci, Linda M. Lemura, Steven L. Cohen, Ethan A. Urbansky, Sara A. Chelland, and Serge P. von Duvillard, "The Effects of Frequency of Encouragement on Performance During Maximal Exercise Testing," *Journal of Sports Sciences* 20, no. 4 (April 2002): 345-352.

Gary Giddins says: Peter Gerler, "The Dozens: King Oliver," *Jazz.com,* http://www.jazz.com/dozens/the-dozens-king-oliver (accessed June 2010).

3 I Get Ideas

Details of Louis Armstrong's experiences with the Karnofskys are found in Louis Armstrong, "Louis Armstrong + the Jewish Family in New Orleans, LA., the Year of 1907," in *Louis Armstrong in His Own Words,* chap. 1.

"The Karnofsky family kept": Ibid., 15-16.

"They were always warm": Ibid., 9.

"I will love": Ibid., 11.

"The best Friend": Ibid., 6.

"He was the least prejudiced musician": George Bornstein, "Satchmo on St. Pat's Day," *Detroit News,* March 17, 2011, 2B.

"White audiences,": Ibid., 11.

Pops was so moved: Jay Smith and Len Guttridge, *Jack Teagarden: The Story of a Jazz Maverick* (Boston: Da Capo Press, 1988), 75.

"Those people who make": Terry Teachout, *Pops* (Boston: Houghton Mifflin Harcourt, 2009), 16.

"Let me tell you something": Bornstein, "Satchmo on St. Pat's Day."

Biographer Terry Teachout believes: Teachout, *Pops,* 144.

1200-item record collection: Michael Cogswell, *Satchmo: The Offstage Story of Louis Armstrong* (Portland, OR: Collectors Press, 2003), 90; Teachout, *Pops,* 291.

In 1968: Teachout, *Pops,* 355.

"Give this son of a gun": Ibid., 281.

recent research: "Speaking Two Languages May Delay Alzheimer's," *NBC News*, http://www.msnbc.msn.com/id/
41670925/ns/health-alzheimers_disease/t/speaking-two-
languages-may-delay-alzheimers (accessed July 2012).

"It was the Jewish family": Armstrong, "Louis Armstrong + the
Jewish Family," 18.

4 Now You Has Jazz

"I dropped the paper": Louis Armstrong, "Jazz on a High Note,"
Esquire 36 (Dec. 1951): 85; quoted in Daniel Stein, *Music Is
My Life: Louis Armstrong, Autobiography, and American Jazz*
(Ann Arbor: University of Michigan Press, 2012), 62.

a helpful online resource: "The Road to Resilience," *American Psychological Association*, http://www.apa.org/helpcenter/
road-resilience.aspx/ (accessed July 2012).

Breathing in, I calm my body: Thich Nhat Hanh, *The Blooming of a
Lotus* (Boston: Beacon Press, 1993), 15.

5 Swing That Music

"Come by starting date": Teachout, *Pops*, 87.

"I had it in my pocket": Ward and Burns, *Jazz*, 134.

"shouldy approach to life": David Burns, *The Feeling Good Hand-
book, revised ed.* (New York: Plume, 1999), 10.

Even among our youth: Sadie F. Dingfelder, "Reflecting on Narcissism: Are Young People More Self-Obsessed Than Ever
Before?" *Monitor on Psychology*, www.apa.org/monitor/
2011/02/narcissism.aspx (accessed August 2011).

doom loop: Jim Collins, *Good to Great: Why Some Companies Make
the Leap and Others Don't* (New York: HarperCollins, 2011),
chap. 8.

He likened his philosophy: Louis Armstrong, "Scanning the History of Jazz," in *Louis Armstrong in His Own Words*, 175.

"The clarion call": Gunther Schuller, *Early Jazz* (Oxford: Oxford
University Press, 1968), 89.

"If you take": Ricky Riccardi, "75 Years of Louis Armstrong's
Unbelievable May 18, 1936, Decca Session," *The Wonderful
World of Louis Armstrong*, http://dippermouth.blogspot

.com/2011/05/75-years-of-louis-armstrongs.html (access-ed August 2011).

6 That's My Home

"Lucille, I might as well": Giddins, *Satchmo*, 115.

"He took one look": Nat Hentoff, *The Jazz Life* (New York: Dial Press, 1961; repr., Boston: Da Capo Press, 1975), 26-27.

"One look at that": Louis Armstrong, "Early Years with Lucille," in *Louis Armstrong in his Own Words*, 144.

650 reel to reel tapes: Many photos of Louis's tape-box collages are found in the marvelous coffee table book, Steven Brower's *Satchmo: The Wonderful World and Art of Louis Armstrong* (New York: Abrams, 2009).

"I love my wife": Louis Armstrong, "Letter to Joe Glaser," in *Louis Armstrong in his Own Words*, 158.

Louis wrote in 1970: Louis Armstrong, "Our Neighborhood," in *Louis Armstrong in his Own Words*, 176-177.

"During my 54 years": Louis Armstrong, "Open Letter to Fans," in *Louis Armstrong in his Own Words*, 183.

Close friend Phoebe Jacobs: Ward and Burns, *Jazz*, 450.

"We don't need": Charles L. Sanders, "Louis Armstrong: The Reluctant Millionaire," *Ebony*, Nov. 1964, 138.

"We've both seen three": Ibid.

a very touching photograph: Ward and Burns, *Jazz*, 452.

"I listened not so much": Ward and Burns, *Jazz*, 316.

7 It's a Most Unusual Day

"The food that you all eat": Giddins, *Satchmo*, 30-31.

"one of my toughest customers": Louis Armstrong, "Open Letter to Fans," *Louis Armstrong in His Own Words*, 181.

"I take my Swiss Kriss": Max Jones & John Chilton, *Louis: The Louis Armstrong Story, 1900-1971* (London: Studio Vista, 1971; repr., Boston: Da Capo Press, 1988), 220.

"Your first dose": Louis Armstrong, "Lose Weight the Satchmo Way," in Bergreen, *An Extravagant Life*, 448-449.

Tony Bennett enjoys: Tony Bennett, in Gary Giddins, *Satchmo*, documentary film, Toby Byron Multiprizes, 1989.

a discussion thread: "Trek T-shirts," *TrekBBS.com*, http://trekbbs

.com/showthread.php?t=99245&highlight=t-shirt (accessed October 2009).

Swiss Kriss Directions: Liberty Hall Jazz Quartet, http://www.libertyhall.com/Stamp/kriss.html (accessed July 2012).

8 Black and Blue

"They wouldn't give up": Louis Armstrong, "Louis Armstrong + the Jewish Family in New Orleans, LA. the Year of 1907," in *Louis Armstrong in His Own Words,* 17.

"I ain't goin' back": "Unconstitutional Law Nixes Satchmo's Mixed Band," *Jet,* Nov. 26, 1959, 56-59.

"There was something": Teachout, *Pops,* 322.

Mr. Armstrong said: Associated Press, "Louis Armstrong, Barring Soviet Tour, Denounces Eisenhower and Gov. Faubus," *New York Times,* September 19, 1957.

We now know; Reaction was mixed: Teachout, *Pops,* 331-332.

Columnist Jim Bishop: Bergreen, *An Extravagant Life,* 318.

Mr. President: Louis Armstrong, Telegram to Dwight D. Eisenhower, Sept. 24, 1957, in *Louis Armstrong in His Own Words,* 194.

"When I see": Brothers, ed., *Louis Armstrong in His Own Words,* 194.

In a wonderful essay: Chuck Klosterman, "My Zombie, Myself: Why Modern Life Feels Rather Undead," *New York Times,* December 3, 2010.

Former Navy SEAL: David Martin, "The Secret SEAL Team That Took Down bin Ladn," *CBS News,* http://www.cbsnews.com/stories/2011/05/06/eveningnews/main20060615.shtml (accessed May 2011).

One important factor: Wendy Wood, Sharon Lundgren, Judith A. Ouellette et al., "Minority Influence: A Meta-Analytic Review of Social Influence Processes, *Psychological Bulletin* 115, no. 3 (May 1994): 323-345.

"Now I want all you people": Ricky Riccardi, *What a Wonderful World: The Magic of Louis Armstrong's Later Years* (New York: Pantheon, 2011), 281.

9 Body and Soul

"life wasn't worth": Teachout, *Pops*, 356.

"Doc, that's all right": Ibid., 367.

"When I pick up that horn": Ibid., 22.

"First comes my horn": Bergreen, *An Extravagant Life*, 421.

"I never tried to prove nothing": Albin Krebs, "Louis Armstrong, Jazz Trumpeter and Singer, Dies," *New York Times*, July 7, 1971.

"Happiness lies at the intersection": Jen Angel, "10 Things Science Says Will Make You Happy," *Yes!* www.yesmagazine.org/ issues/sustainable-happiness/10-things-science-says-will-make-you (accessed August 2011).

"Pops loved to play": Teachout, *Pops*, 348.

"You ever give me a night off": Riccardi, *What a Wonderful World*, 244-245.

Clarinetist Joe Darensbourg: Ibid., 211.

10 What a Wonderful World

Record producer Bob Thiele: Teachout, *Pops*, 351.

The head of the label: Riccardi, *What a Wonderful World*, 260.

"a smile that came from within": "Reliving the Legend of Louis Armstrong," *CNN.com*, http://premium.asia.cnn.com/ TRANSCRIPTS/0108/04/smn.16.html (accessed June 2012).

"My whole life": Teachout, *Pops*, 379.

"People love me": Giddins, *Satchmo*, 83.

spending twenty dollars: Dacher Keltner, *Born to Be Good* (W. W. Norton & Company, 2009), 5.

In an experiment: Frans de Waal, "The Evolution of Empathy," *Greater Good*, http://greatergood.berkeley.edu/article/ item/the_evolution_of_empathy (accessed June 2012).

They get their soul lifted: Riccardi, *What a Wonderful World*, 306.

George Avakian said: "Reliving the Legend," CNN.

Late in Louis's life: Ward and Burns, *Jazz*, 453.

"I've had a beautiful life": Riccardi, *What a Wonderful World*, 281.

"I'm too busy thinking": Michael Rosenberg, "We All Have a Shot at Happiness," *Detroit Free Press*, http://www.freep .com/article/20120518/COL22/205180431/michael-rosenberg-ford-field-elevator (accessed May 2012).

"What is the use": "Quotes Falsely Attributed," *Winston Churchill Centre and Museum*, http://www.winstonchurchill .org/learn/speeches/quotations/quotes-falsely-attributed (accessed June 2012).

Coda

And all I'm saying: Louis Armstrong, spoken introduction to "What a Wonderful World," *Louis Armstrong and His Friends*, LP 6369401, Phillips, 1970.

Photographs

Frontispiece: Herman Hiller, *New York World-Telegram & Sun,* 1953, public domain.
73: New York World-Telegram & Sun, 1953, public domain.
97: Joseph P. Gottlieb, 1946, public domain.
134: Joseph P. Gottlieb, 1947, public domain.
168: Original image by "Hephaestos," *Wikimedia Commons,* http://commons.wikimedia.org/wiki/File: BlueberryiBook.jpeg (accessed July 2012), Creative Commons Attribution-Share Alike 3.0 license.

About the Author

Phil Lynch is author of the motivational blog UpTeach (upteach.blogspot.com), the leading site of encouragement for educators. He holds a degree in psychology from the University of Michigan and a master's degree in history from Fort Hays State University, Kansas. A former United Methodist youth pastor, Phil is a psychology and social studies instructor with over twenty years' experience helping students reach their potential in the Escanaba, Michigan, public schools.

Phil is also a lifelong musician, having received in high school – as a bit of foreshadowing – the Louis Armstrong Jazz Award. In his spare time he's a semi-professional jazz pianist scouring the backwoods of Michigan's Upper Peninsula for gigs with his trio. He resides in Escanaba, on the north shore of Lake Michigan, with his wife and four children.

Made in the USA
Monee, IL
10 January 2022

87654505R00104